JERUSALEM

Bridging
the Four Walls

A Geopolitical Perspective

by Saul B. Cohen

Herzl Press

New York

Library of Congress Catalog Card No. 77-76665

Printed in the U.S.A.

This book is dedicated to my wife Miriam who has encouraged my various works abroad, particularly those connected with Jerusalem.

CONTENTS

Figures, Tables and Photographic Perspectives

Table

7

Acknowledgements

Over the years, my studies in Jerusalem have been stimulated by contacts with friends and colleagues who have guided my explorations within the city, have provided me with access to its materials and have imbued me with their sense of its spirituality. Professor David Amiran of the Department of Geography at the Hebrew University is a continuing source of personal inspiration and support. Other valued geographer-colleagues, Yehoshua Ben Arieh, Amiram Gonen, Shalom Reichman and Arieh Shachar, have shared Jerusalem with me from their topical perspectives. The departmental base that I enjoy when teaching and pursuing research in Jerusalem has been a most useful resource.

Another stimulus for this book is my work with Professor Alex Weingrod of the Anthropology Department, University of the Negev, and Professors Amiran and Shachar at the Jerusalem Studies Center of the Institute of Urban and Regional Studies, the Hebrew University. The focus of this Center is contemporary social scientific research on Israel.

For specific help in developing materials useful to the writing of the volume, I wish to thank: Miriam Karmon of the Hebrew University Geography Department; Israel Kimchi, Head of the Policy Planning and Research Branch of the Jerusalem City Planning Department; and Aharon Davidi and Avshalom Shmueli of the Geography faculty at Tel Aviv University.

Warm thanks are due for the technical support received at Clark University. Herbert Heidt, Manager of the School of Geography's Cartography Laboratory gave generously of his time in map design and production, and Bruce Meier provided design advice, while Alan Savada and David Selden volunteered their time and experience unstintingly in map research and compilation. Mary O'Malley, the School's administrator, her associates Johnette Ebbeling and Evelyn Larson, and Theresa Reynolds, Supervisor of the Clark Secretarial Pool, saw the manuscript through its various drafts. I also am deeply appreciative of the efforts of Lynne Goldstein of the Herzl Press in New York. She not only provided editorial assistance but steered the volume through its various technical publication phases.

Herman Jenkins, my graduate student and colleague, volunteered his combined artistry and cartographic skills in presenting "The Four Walls of Jerusalem". He succeeded in articulating with pen and ink what otherwise would have remained an author's idea. Photographs in the two photographic essays, "Perspectives of East Jerusalem's Israeli Housing Estates" and "Perspectives of the Four Walls of Jerusalem," were taken by Werner Braun, the Jerusalem photographer. His skills, patience, imagination and experiential knowledge have been the basis for adding an important photographic dimension to the volume, and I am indeed grateful.

A very special expression of thanks is owed my sister-in-law, Lillian F. Blacker. She combined her grasp of history, her critical literary facilities and her professional editorial skills in helping me to prepare this volume for publication.

Finally, I want to express my indebtedness to Edward Parsons of Kibbutz Kfar Blum in Israel. Over the years he has been mentor, guide and teacher to me. He has inspired my studies on Israel and maintained a dialogue which provokes continuing reexamination of basic objectives and underlying assumptions in my research. His searching questions have helped provide direction for this volume.

Publication of this book coincides with the marking of a decade of Jerusalem's unity, after nineteen painful years of partition. It is my hope that the geopolitical perspective within which I have examined Jerusalem will contribute to the search for a solution to the Jerusalem problem within the framework of continued unity. A unified city under Israeli sovereignty can and must provide for the pluralism of national, communal and spiritual interests that give Jerusalem its uniqueness. A unified city also offers Israel a unique measure of strategic security. Assurance of this strategic position would enable Israel to take the initiative in breaking the current political deadlock, by offering the Arabs an opportunity to develop a West Bank entity. Israeli Jerusalem, sensitive to the needs for far-reaching autonomy of non-Jewish and, indeed, Jewish citizens, and completely open to the West Bank as well as the rest of Israel, can link Arabs and Jews in a unique way, contributing substantially to eventual resolution of the Arab-Israeli conflict.

Jerusalem's Central Importance in the Arab-Israeli Conflict

"The struggle for Jerusalem will determine the fate not only of the country but of the Jewish people." (Prime Minister David Ben Gurion, 1948).

"It (Jerusalem) holds a special position for every Muslim nation because of the Arab, Kurdish, Circassion and Turkish blood which has been shed on its behalf throughout the history of Islam." (King 'Abdallah, 1951).

"A second and very important step, particularly in view of the prospect of the virtual destruction of this historic city that belongs to the whole world, would be an order for the demilitarization of the city of Jerusalem as a whole." (Count Folke Bernadotte, 1948).[1]

No other city in the world has been subject to such intense competition for control as Jerusalem during its 4,000 years of recorded history. The religious interests of the three world faiths for whom Jerusalem is so paramount can be fulfilled without their having to hold territorial control of the city. But territorial control is an overriding issue for the two nationalisms, Arab and Jewish, whose governments are in contention for the city. In the struggle of nationalisms sovereign space cannot be shared, although some sharing of political power is possible.

11

During most of its history, Jerusalem was territorially united under the political authority that dominated the entire country. Only in the nineteenth and twentieth centuries (and during the Third Crusade) were political structures developed which attempted to share the city in some fashion. Ottoman concessions to European powers, providing for European responsibilities for Christian Holy Places, is an example of a sharing mechanism. Stillborn plans to internationalize the city, brought forward first during British Mandatory times and then within the forum of the United Nations are also examples. The 1948-1967 partition of Jerusalem between Israel and Jordan is still another form of territorial sharing or division.

None of the foregoing strategems are applicable today to solving the Jerusalem problems, because no simple, single-functional mechanism can satisfy all of the conflicting needs. Instead, a multi-faceted approach is required which will adapt the political status of the city to its complex geopolitical and cultural realities. First and foremost among the realities is nationalism. While the religious claims upon Jerusalem of Jews, Arabs and Christians are universalistic in philosophy, the nationalistic claims of Israelis and Palestinian Arabs are particularistic. They relate to the specific role and importance of the city relative to other parts of the actual or potential national territories. Israelis have already decided they will not barter their control of Jerusalem for the *promise* of peace. Palestinian Arabs have yet to decide whether they should barter their claims in Jerusalem for a *guaranteed* West Bank national entity.

Various suggestions on Jerusalem's future have been put forward, especially in the years immediately following the reunification of the city on June 7, 1967. Many proposals were initiated by the Israelis, but never tested in an action setting. Israel has pursued a policy of deferring the Jerusalem question until other aspects of the conflict — territorial boundaries, the refugees, the political status of the West Bank — have been solved.

Time, however, is against continued deferral of the Jerusalem problem, as it is against the delay of a general framework for peace. Consequences of the War of October, 1973, and the growth of Arab military and political strength since then require that initiative on Jerusalem be taken by the one party to the conflict that can do so — Israel.

Proposals for a Jerusalem settlement should be based upon the salience of Israeli and Arab Palestinian nationalism as forces that shape and perpetuate the conflict. A realistic proposal must also take into account the need for sharing of political power. Sharing does not and cannot imply territorial division between sovereignties, but sharing should mean giving to the various peoples of Jerusalem an unprecedented degree of formal political autonomy at the municipal, submunicipal and metropolitan levels.

The premise that a new geopolitical structure for Jerusalem must develop within a unified Israeli territorial framework, stems from the view of the Arab-Israeli conflict as being both ideological and territorial. These two concepts are not separate; they are intertwined. On the one hand, Jewish, Muslim and Christian attitudes are bound up with the spiritual notion of territory as a holy land. On the other hand, the national territorial changes that have already occurred in the modern Holy Land influence the ideological goals of the contending groups. New territorial changes will cause a reshaping of ideological goals, just as ideology will set limits on the capacities of the conflicting forces to accept boundary shifts.

THREE STAGES OF PARTITION

The Jerusalem issue should be considered within the general context of the succession of territorial changes that have occurred in Palestine through both diplomatic and military actions. This places the focus squarely on the setting of contending nationalisms.

Territorial changes in Palestine and Israel are part of a process of conflict and compromise which has been occurring for more than half a century. The initial stage of compromise began with the first Partition of Palestine in 1922. The Cairo Conference then affirmed the Churchill White Paper's establishment of Transjordan.[2] Formally confirmed as an Emirate in 1925, the land east of the Jordan was closed to Jewish settlement. Transjordan represented 76% of the total land area of the Palestine Mandate, and the land that retained the name Palestine now was approximately one-third of Biblical Palestine.

In fact, Zionist leaders never seriously entertained the notion of settling in all of what was to become Transjordan. In 1919, for example, Zionists presented a settlement-plan that was based upon the lines of the Israelite settlement of Solomon's kingdom (See Figure 1).[3] The Zionist plan contained much of Biblical Edom, Moab and Ammon, including the hot steppe climatic region (over 200 mm. annual rainfall) of modern-day Jordan, as well as the Dead Sea-Arava reaches. Its eastern boundary lay just west of the Hejaz railway, on which were situated Amman, Deraa and Maan. As in the Solomonic Kingdom, the Golan, Mount Hermon and the Lower Litani River were included in the plan. So were Philistia (Jaffa to Gaza) and the northern Palestinian coast (Tyre to Acre), over which Solomon never succeeded in gaining control.

Meinertzhagen, in 1919, had proposed substantially the same area for Palestine, save for a northern boundary that followed the northern shore of the Lower Litani (rather than including the entire basin almost to Sidon).[4] By suggesting a boundary that included both banks of the Litani River up to the Litani gorges, and then including those of the Hermon waters which flow into the Litani or Jordan basins, Meinertzhagen sought to assure Palestine of control of its essential water sources — a matter of vital concern to the Zionists.[5] Southeast of the Dead Sea, he suggested a slightly narrower strip of land to the Gulf of Aqaba just east of the town of Aqaba (See Figure 1).

The northern boundary of Palestine proved a point of considerable contention between the British and the French. The French wished to base the boundary on the Sykes-Picot Agreement, continuing east beyond the Sea of Galilee across the Yarmuk Valley to Deraa. The British sought a line that followed the Lower Litani thalweg to the bend of the river and then to Banias, Wadi al Muganiye and the western end of the Leja region. After several years of negotiation and change, the line was fixed in 1922-23 (See Figure 2). It extended east from Ras en Nakura, then turned north to Metullah, east to Banias and south to include the Jordan headwaters as they flow through the Hule Basin. The western part of the Golan Heights, treated as part of Palestine in the French-British Agreement of 1920, was detached, while the French gave up their claim to the Hule Basin and to a small area along the northern frontier, north of Sasa.

The second stage of territorial compromise began with a series of partition plans formally or informally put forward as early as

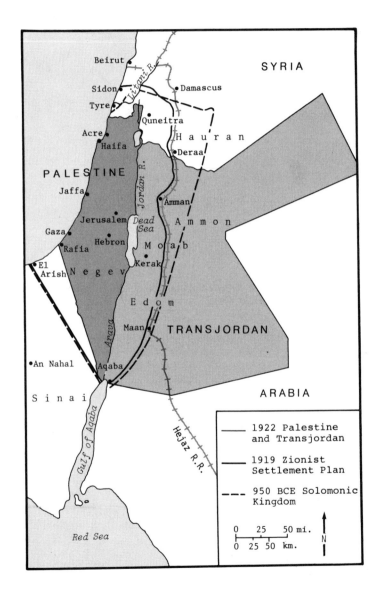

Fig. 1. The Different Palestines

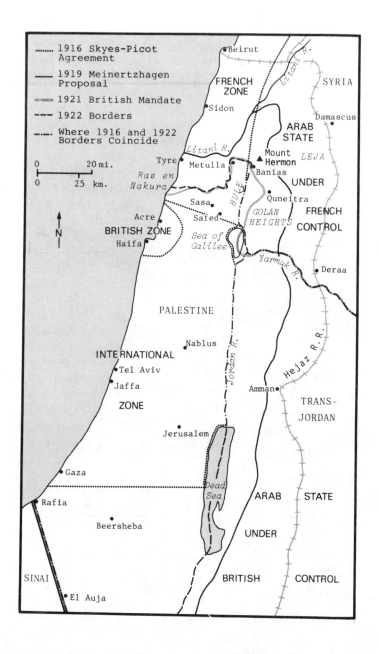

Fig. 2. Palestine's Boundaries — Early Twentieth Century

1932; was brought to a head by the United Nations Palestine Partition Plan of November 29, 1947; and culminated in the Armistice Agreements with Egypt, Lebanon, Jordan and Syria of February-July, 1949.[6] As a result of the process of negotiation, war and renegotiation, the Jewish territorial base at the end of this second stage included approximately 20% of the total land area of the original Palestine Mandate, and 40% of the territory to which Zionist leaders had hoped the Balfour Declaration would apply. On the other hand, the new state now had a total of 26,000 square kilometers, or about one and one-half times the area alloted to the Jewish state in the United Nations Plan (See Figure 3).

The third stage of the partitioning process began in 1967 with Israel's occupation of the West Bank, Gaza, all of the Sinai and the Golan Heights, several years later followed by modest withdrawals in the Sinai and the Golan (See Figure 4). This period has already been marked by three wars: the Six Day War of 1967; the War of Attrition of 1969-70; and the Yom Kippur War of 1973. The stage is also characterized by: global diplomatic struggles in such agencies as the United Nations, UNESCO and the I.L.O.; economic boycotts by Arab oil producing countries against those nations allied with Israel, and the Arab boycott against firms and individuals that do business with Israel; conflicts in adjoining territories — the Palestinian-Jordanian hostilities of 1970, the Lebanese War of 1975-76; international terror and Palestinian guerilla actions within Israel, and Israeli counter-strikes; and formal negotiations such as the First and Second Sinai Agreements between Israel and Egypt, January 18, 1974, and September 1, 1975, and the Israeli-Syrian Agreement along the Golan Heights in May 31, 1974.[7]

The process is still going on, and it is inexorable. Ultimately a new territorial partition will evolve that will have to strike a more mutually acceptable compromise between the boundaries of 1949 and those of 1967. While some obvious forces — comparative military might, superpower intercession, the nature of the specific agreement (cease-fire, nonbelligerency, or peace) — will determine the location of the line, other less predictable forces will also play a role. These include the ultimate consequences of the Lebanese conflict, whether status quo ante, partition into Christian and Muslim states, or de facto control by Syria; and the strength and durability of the efforts to forge a Syrian-Jordanian

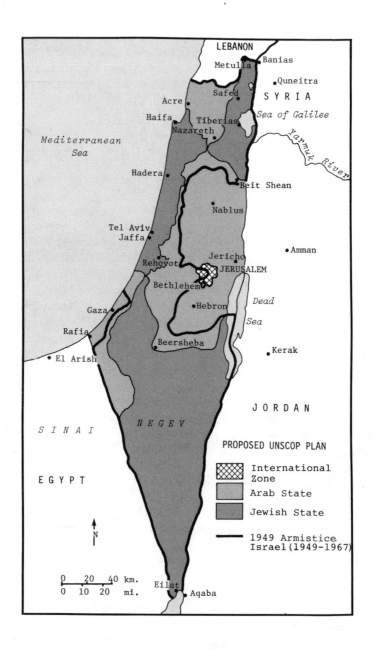

Fig. 3. UNSCOP and 1949 Armistice Boundaries

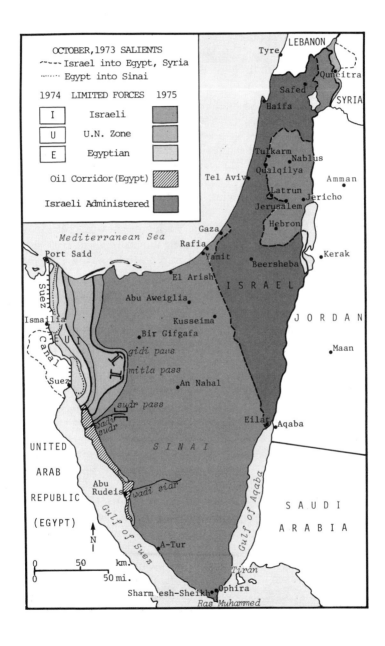

Fig. 4. Israel and the Administered Territories

alliance. Of particular significance to the Arab-Israeli conflict would be the emergence of a federation between Syria and Jordan, and a possible commitment to broaden such a federation to include the Palestinian West Bank.

Whatever the outcome of this third partition stage, it is not likely to be the last one in territorial rearrangement. For a new partition that does not have as its quid pro quo a formal peace between the Arabs and the Israelis, including a resolution of the Palestinian refugee problem, will contain the seeds of conflict renewal. However, partition accepted as an element of a genuine peace between the warring peoples would, in all likelihood, be followed by a new territorial stage that builds upon this formal peace. This could take the form of a federative framework between Israel and the Arab states. Such a framework could help to maximize the spiritual and economic capabilities of both peoples through positive interaction, and would eliminate territorial disjunctions in a functional if not formal way through free-trade zones, transit corridors, or unification of villages.

JERUSALEM AS THE CENTRAL TERRITORIAL ISSUE

In the third and current stage of territorial compromise, the issue of Jerusalem is likely to become the central territorial issue. The focus of this volume is on modern Jerusalem's geopolitical present and future. What happens to Jerusalem should be seen within the context of an unfolding stage of more general territorial compromise.

A break in the current stalemate of the Arab-Israeli conflict may come through diplomatic or military means. Peaceful alternatives include a third-phase Israeli withdrawal in the Sinai in exchange for formal Egyptian nonbelligerency; far-reaching territorial concessions in the Golan for formal Syrian nonbelligerency; or the linking of retreat from the Sinai, alteration in the status of the Golan, and return of much of the West Bank to a secure peace. A resumption of hostilities might occur as an unforeseen consequence of the recent conflict in Lebanon. War might erupt as a result of direct Israeli intervention to keep the Palestinians from regaining control of Southern Lebanon; or the Syrian-Israeli conflict might be resumed if Syria succeeds in absorbing Lebanon within its sphere of influence and threatens Israel from both the Golan and Southern Lebanon. An Israeli victory in such a war could result in formal military occupation by Israel of Southern Lebanon up to the Litani River. But no matter what the course of short-term events, the long-range prospects are for a rollback of the Israeli presence from most of the territories gained since June of 1967.

Israeli attitudes towards the ultimate disposition of additions to the 1967 cease-fire borders have been ambivalent and ambiguous. Changing governmental policies reflect negotiation strategies and external pressures, as well as the political seesaw on which are balanced "minimalists" of various ideological hues, and "maximalists", who adhere to Eretz Israel HaShelemah (undivided Israel) for either ideological or security reasons.

In most of the recent Israeli discussions over the future of the territories, a firm "no negotiation" posture has been adopted on the issue of Jerusalem. Although Jerusalem has been on the diplomatic "back burner," with recent attention being on the Sinai, the Golan, Southern Lebanon, and, increasingly, on the West Bank, ultimately, Jerusalem will prove the greatest bone of territorial contention between Israel and the Arabs. The current Israeli policy of maintaining control over a united Jerusalem will be the greatest obstacle to an Arab formal agreement on a permanent peace. Paradoxically, a unified Israeli Jerusalem could, in the long run, help secure enduring peace by serving to link Israel and a Palestinian state in geopolitically functional terms.

TWO GEOGRAPHICAL LEVELS OF CONFLICT

This may be better understood by viewing the Arab-Israeli conflict as taking place at two geographical levels: internal (Jews versus the Arabs in former Palestine), and external (Israel versus the Arab states). The conflict within Israel, the West Bank and what was "Fatahland," especially guerrilla activity and small scale military response, occurs in or near heavily populated Jewish areas. The scene of the external conflict, in which are arrayed massed armed forces, is removed from Jewish centers of population—along the Golan Heights, the Jordan River Valley and in the Sinai. Prior to the War of 1967, the two forms of contention took place within Palestine in the same geographical arenas; now they are spatially separated, even though linked politically and ideologically.

Most of the outside world, including Israel's Western friends, have, by espousing various United Nations resolutions calling for Israel's return of territories occupied in June of 1967, assumed that peace can only be achieved through essentially a return to coterminous contention boundaries — the external and the internal. Israel's policy objective, in contrast, is to prevent a geographical relinking of the military positions of the Arab states and the operational bases of the Palestinian guerrillas within or at Israel's borders.

Various arguments over what territorial concessions Israel can afford to make often fail to distinguish clearly between the two different levels of contention. But the strategic implications to Israel of yielding territory in the Sinai and in the Golan are considerably different from the implications of abandoning military and settlement presences within the "green line" of the West Bank or surrounding Gaza.

With respect to its external, Arab state geographical relations, Israel may well be able to work out accommodations with Egypt, Syria, Jordan, and in Lebanon. Her viability as a state would not be threatened if mutual concessions were made, linking territorial compromises to: political declarations of recognition and nonbelligerency; limitations of armaments and disposition of armed forces; establishment of demilitarized zones; assurance of international water passageways; outside power guarantees of the status quo.

With respect to internal relations, however, Israel can scarcely make territorial concessions without undermining her viability as a state. The tactical securing of boundaries holds for the Gaza and Qualkilya-Latrun reaches adjoining Israel's Central region, but it especially applies to the Jerusalem city-region and the Corridor. Jerusalem is the strategic fulcrum for Israeli-Palestinian Arab relations in the West Bank as a whole. Outside powers trying to advance negotiations for a Middle Eastern peace should keep in mind the lack of symmetry between the strategic significance to Israel of the Sinai and the Golan, and the strategic significance to Israel of a united, expanded Jerusalem region. There can be no peace without self-determination for West Bank Palestinians, either in independent fashion or linked to a broader

Arab entity. But there also can be no peace without Israel's securing Jerusalem as a strategic hedge against the emergence of a West Bank political entity that could constitute a serious military threat.

CHANGING EMPHASIS UPON JERUSALEM AMONG THE THREE RELIGIONS

That the three traditions, Jewish, Christian and Islamic, have centuries-old links to Jerusalem and fundamental stakes in its future is undeniable, although, as Colin Williams has pointed out, Jerusalem has a far more powerful corporate meaning for Judaism than for Christianity and Islam.[8] Christians have Rome and Muslims have Mecca, but Jews have only Jerusalem. Nevertheless, for each religion, Jerusalem plays a central role in concept, ritual and emotion. These links and stakes, unbroken through time and with mystical significance and symbolisms, may prove even more eternal than the stones and mortar of the "eternal" city. They operate, however, within a real world context. This is the world of the people who live within or visit Jerusalem, the armies that stand over it, and the political authorities and the economic stewards who determine its material destinies. As Jerusalem's real world context changes, the depth of feeling and interpretation of the spiritual ties of each tradition adapt to this changing milieu.

For Christians, Jerusalem during the Byzantine Period (324-638 A.D.) may not have been more salient spiritually than it was during the Arab period (638-1071 A.D.) but the notion of Jerusalem's physical centrality, so strongly held during the first period, was subdued during the second.[9] When Emperor Constantine took control of Palestine in 324 A.D., he initiated the building of churches, including the Church of the Holy Sepulcher, that gave to the city a Christian character. Succeeding emperors expanded the Christian landscape through their construction of churches and monastaries, and Christian pilgrims from all over the world flocked to Jerusalem. During much of this time Jews were banned from the city.

The other period of major Christian emphasis upon Jerusalem was the First Crusader Kingdom (1099-1187). Religious and secular bodies were established in the city and a major wave of church building took place, including the Citadel.

Jews and Muslims were banished, and tens of thousands of European Christian pilgrims poured into Jerusalem each year. During the Third Crusader occupation of the city (1229-44), the Christians did not succeed in settling the city or developing its economic life on the grand scale of the First Jerusalem Kingdom.

Within Islam, Jerusalem enjoyed an especially flourishing role as a religious center during the Omayyad Dynasty (660-750 A.D.), during part of the Mameluke era (which extended in Jerusalem from 1260-1516), and in the very first few years of the Ottoman rule (during the reign of the Sultan Suleiman the Magnificent from 1520-66).[10] In the Omayyad period, Abd-el-Malik erected the Dome of the Rock and the Aqsa edifices which became the Harem-esh-Sharif. The Mamelukes did very little to develop Jerusalem's economy, but constructed large numbers of mosques, religious colleges and hospices for Islamic pilgrims. Suleiman the Magnificent rebuilt Jerusalem's wall and gates (1537-41), refurbished the Dome of the Rock and the Citadel, and developed the city's water supply. The Sultan dedicated many properties to the support of Jerusalem's colleges and hospices.

On the other hand, during the Baghdadi-based Abbasid rule that followed the Omayyad dynasty (750-941), and during much of the Ottoman hegemony prior to the nineteenth century, respect lessened for the city's central role within Islam. This was expressed particularly in Jerusalem's decline as a center for Muslim learning and pilgrimage. Even during the Omayyad period, Jerusalem showed early signs of decline in importance when the Sultan Suleiman founded Ramleh and made it the capital of the province of Falastin. But under the Abassids, Jerusalem was allowed to fall into disrepair, not even to be visited by some of the Caliphs. Ramleh, on the other hand, received considerable attention, in the form of walls, its mosque and waterworks.[11]

The Ottoman period that was initiated by such a large-scale construction effort, was largely characterized by lack of attention to Jerusalem's development. Because it was strategically unimportant to the Turks and politically down-graded, and because it attracted no permanent Turkish population, Jerusalem had a very low profile within Islam. In the nineteenth century,

Christians began to take a strong renewed interest in the Holy Land, partly because of England's and France's economic interests in the Middle East. With development of Christian and Jewish places of worship and shrines, Muslims, too, began to pay renewed attention to their religious edifices in the Old City.

For Judaism, Jerusalem has continuously retained its central mythic role, and the belief that humankind's redemption could only be expected after the return of Jewish political control to Jerusalem and restoration of the Temple. Yet even within Judaism, adaptations to Jerusalem's political environment were made.[12] The appeal of Jerusalem to Jews was muted during Byzantine and later Crusader times. But the promise of future fulfillment through the restoration of Jerusalem became especially salient for Jewish pilgrims during the Fatimid Dynasty (969-1071). During that period, competition within Jerusalem between the Rabbanites and the Karaites served to strengthen the general Jewish focus on the Holy City. Another period in which Jerusalem played a strong central role was with the Messianic movements of the 16th and 17th centuries, when the loose Ottoman reign held sway in the Holy City.

In the latter part of the nineteenth century, Jerusalem experienced modernization and a stronger central authority offered equal rights to non-Muslims. Jews took advantage of the new political environment. They expressed their yearnings for Jerusalem by moving to it in large numbers. Expansion of Jerusalem's religious educational institutions was partly at the expense of the Holy Cities of Safed and Tiberias, from which the Jewish population had fled when the towns were leveled by earthquakes in the early nineteenth century.

It is difficult to separate religious feelings from the political environment. Many of the religious energies inherent in the three religions are latent. They require a special set of historical, material circumstances to energize them. If spirituality is the sacred, and materialism is the profane, they are not in this sense contradictory, but rather have a synergistic relationship. Up to the end of the nineteenth century, the role of religion was primary in shaping the city's landscape characteristics and in affecting its growth patterns.[13] Even today there is no disputing the importance of the city because it is holy to the three monotheistic religions. Nonetheless, contemporary political events suggest political solutions to the Jerusalem issue which address religious feelings separately from geopolitical realities. To make such a distinction is not easy, for Jerusalem's spiritual significance to Jews, Muslims and Christians is generally the starting point for discussions about its present role and future disposition.

For Jews not only of Israel but of the world, the division of Jerusalem from 1949 to 1967, attended by the denial to Jews of access to the Old City, and by the destruction or desecration of Arab-held Jewish holy sites and living quarters, became an unacceptable dimension of the Arab-Israeli conflict. For Arabs throughout the Middle East, the post-1967 unification and physical expansion of Jerusalem, attended by the loss of control over Arab holy sites, has made the future of Jerusalem a central issue in the conflict. For many Christians, especially Roman Catholics represented by the Vatican, national territorial status for Jerusalem, be this status Israeli/Jordanian or fully Israeli, has remained far less desirable than some form of internationalization. This is the logical consequence of a Christian view of Jerusalem as a place whose uniqueness for Christians can best be safeguarded, if no longer through the establishment of a Crusader-like kingdom of the Middle Ages, then at least as an internationally-administered city, or as a city with extraterritorial status for its religious sites.

Religious feelings about Jerusalem are, therefore, deep, persistent and tenaciously held by all parties concerned. However, an even more fundamental element is the geopolitical, in which the Christian world now has little stake. For Israelis and Arabs the conflict over Jerusalem is a conflict for control of strategic space — a struggle that is not so much a consequence of broader issues in the conflict, as it is a mirror of this conflict. Jerusalem is the territorial imperative upon which Israel's raison d'etre as a strategically-viable eastern Mediterranean state is based. For the Arabs of the West Bank, Israel's security is their insecurity, as long as they persist in denying Israel's right to exist. No Palestinian state, West Bank or combined Jordanian-West Bank, is defensible territorially without control or neutralization of Jerusalem.

A GEOPOLITICAL SYSTEM OF TWO ORDERS

A unified Jerusalem is evolving as a system of two orders: one, a subsystem of the Israeli national geopolitical system; the other, as a special-type system linking both Israel and the Palestinian Arab West Bank. This evolution casts the Jerusalem issue in a fundamentally different light, not merely from other territories which prior to June 1967 were in Arab hands, but from what Jerusalem itself was prior to its formal reunification as part of Israel's national space.

The Jerusalem city-region has shown remarkable development as a region, a development which follows the organismic-developmental principles that characterize the growth and maturing of a general system. The system is highly complex, differentiated and integrated, both as a system unto itself and as a subsystem of Israel and of the West Bank. From two cities to one city, from a municipality to a city-region, from an area moderately open to outside influences to one that is highly open (flow of migrants, daily labor, tourists, capital, ideas) — the integrated system that is Jerusalem has acquired a life and status of its own. This makes its disposition far less amenable to the dictates of external mediators than was the case in 1947-48 or in 1967.

What characterizes a developed system's ability to achieve integration above all is its feedback mechanisms. Prior to 1967, these were relatively weak. The Jordanians were insensitive to the needs of Arab Jerusalem as a subsystem of the Jordanian Kingdom, and West Jerusalem was a weak appendage of the Jewish national state. Today, there are a variety of forces operating within Jerusalem that influence Israel's national policy, rather than accepting it passively. Chief among them are: the rise in a very powerful Jerusalemite "consciousness" among both traditional and non-observant Jews; the dependence of important sectors of the city's economy upon a large West Bank labor pool; and the increasingly interlocking nature of Jewish and Arab work patterns. Residence and commerce remain more clearly segregated, although in East Jerusalem Arab and Jewish residential areas now adjoin one another.

The attitudes and policies of the Jerusalem Jewish élite towards the development of the city are based on equalization of municipal services, employment and educational opportunities, and on maintenance of social and cultural pluralism. Nowhere else in Israel do Arabs and Jews face one another in such large numbers and so fully as equals, as in Jerusalem. Jerusalem's municipal politics do not mirror Israeli national political trends and debates, but reflect the more unique situation of Israelis and Arabs working together and living next to one another. In spite of tensions and provocations that arise from the general pressures of the Arab-Israeli conflict, this commitment to Jerusalem's unity remains a dominant and powerful force.

Jerusalem's Arabs have a very influential role to play in molding and shaping Arab-Israeli relations. Understandably they take an equivocal stand on the issue of the unity of the city. On the one hand, they strongly voice their Palestinian national aspirations for freedom from Israeli rule; on the other hand, they recognize and value the advantages of the city's unity. Because Jerusalem is so closely linked to Samaria and Judea, the Arabs of Jerusalem have a unique opportunity to help forge a special order of city-region system that seeks co-existence with Jerusalem's other order as a sub-system of Israel. If Jerusalem can remain an integrated arena for Arab-Israeli interaction, then it can continue to serve as a major feedback mechanism in developing policies between Israel and Palestinian Arabs on the future of the West Bank.

Finally, as a new geopolitical system evolves, the landscape takes on new political and cultural values. Jerusalem, the reflection of the past, mirrors the future. The Walled City remains, but its function has rapidly altered, decreasing in residential importance, increasing, relatively, in religious, commercial and tourist significance. The rest of the city has changed in rapid-fire fashion: suburbanization of former rural Arab villages; growth of modern, prosperous Arab suburbs; development of massive Israeli peripheral housing in East Jerusalem; expansion of national governmental, educational, hotel, and commercial facilities; building of industrial zones, and enlargement of road and other communication networks. These elements, like signs, lights, parks, and such cultural expressions as food, dress, language and social spirit, make for a "new"Jerusalem. It is this "new" Jerusalem that is a reality with which Israel, the Arabs and the Christian world must deal.

FOOTNOTES

1. David Ben Gurion, *Israel, A Personal History,* translated from the Hebrew by
    N. Meyers and U. Nystar, New York: Funk & Wagnalls, Inc., 1971, p. 153. An
    address to the Provisional State Council on June 17, during the first truce of
    the War of Independence, dwelling on the struggle for Jerusalem in the
    month before the truce and condemning the Christian world for failing to
    prevent the Arab attack on the Holy City.

    King 'Abdallah of Jordan, *My Memoirs Completed, (al-TaKmilah),* trans-
    lated from the Arabic by Harold W. Glidden. Washington, D.C.: American
    Council of Learned Societies, 1954, p. 22. A description of unsuccessful at-
    tempts by King 'Abdallah during the first truce to persuade Egypt and Iraq to
    join with the Jordanians in a concerted attack to capture all of Jerusalem.

    Folke Bernadotte, *To Jerusalem,* translated from the Swedish by J. Bul-
    man. London: Hodder and Stoughton, 1951, p. 170. Address by the Mediator
    to the Security Council during the July 12-17, 1948 session. The suggestion to
    demilitarize Jerusalem followed the Mediator's abortive proposal made on
    June 27/28 during the first truce to the Arab League Committee and to Israel,
    that the city of Jerusalem be included in Arab territory and entrusted to
    Transjordan. Response of the Israeli Provincial Government in a note of July
    5 was critical to the suggestions in general and was especially bitter about the
    proposal to impose Arab domination on Jerusalem.

2. The 1892 transfer of the North Sinai coast from Turkey to British-controlled
    Egypt may be viewed as a prelude to the first partition phase. The area
    transferred was a triangle from El Arish to the tip of the Gulf of Suez to Port
    Said on the Mediterranean. In 1906, the rest of the Sinai was ceded by Turkey
    to Egypt under pressure from the British. The boundary between Egypt and
    Palestine extended from Rafia to the Gulf of Aqaba and was known as the
    "Administrative Separation Line". (See Col. Richard Meinertzhagen, *Mid-
    dle East Diary, 1917-1956,* New York: Thomas Yoseloff, 1959, p. 64.)

3. The Zionist Organization submitted a territorial plan for Palestine to the
    Paris Peace Conference in February of 1919 that was rejected. What promp-
    ted this initiative was the Sykes-Picot Agreement of May, 1916 (also aban-
    doned at the Paris Peace Conference), which gave the French control of the
    area from a line north of Acre to the northern end of the Sea of Galilee, and
    reserved the Negev (a line from south of Gaza to the Dead Sea) for an Arab
    state under British protection. The Sykes-Picot plan proposed Palestine's
    organization as international (a condominium), with an undefined role for
    Russia and direct control of the Acre and Gaza ports by Britain.

    Zionist fears about the truncation of Palestine were further confirmed
    when a temporary military occupation boundary was set in September of
    1919, from Ras en Nakura to Lake Hule. This left the Hule Basin Jewish
    settlements (Metullah, Kfar Giladi, Hamarah and Tel Hai) outside the sphere
    of British military protection. These settlements fell prey to attacking Arab
    bands, when the French failed to establish military control of this area during
    the Arab rebellion against their occupation of Syria. The four settlements
    were briefly abandoned in 1920 after the battle of Tel Hai in which the Arabs
    were repulsed but Joseph Trumpledor was killed. In May of 1920, the French

29

agreed to return the Galilee "finger" to British supervision. (See Yehuda Wallach, *Atlas Karta L'Toldot Eretz Yisrael Mireishit HaHityashvut V'Ad Kom HaMedina,* (Hebrew) Jerusalem: Karta, 1972, pp. 40-41.

4. Col. Richard Meinertzhagen, *Middle East Diary, 1917-1956, op. cit.,* pp. 61-53. 61-53.

5. In an address to the British Zionist Federation in London in September, 1919, Chaim Weizmann said, "The boundaries of the land must be fixed in such a manner that every drop of water necessary for irrigation of the soil shall flow within its boundaries."

6. Official Records of the Second Session of the General Assembly, Supplement No. 11, *United Nations Special Committee on Palestine – Report to the General Assembly.* Lake Success, New York: A/364, September 3, 1947, Volume I, 65 pp., and A/364, Add. 1, September 9, 1947, Volume II, 64 pp. and maps. The Israel-Arab Armistice Agreements were signed at Rhodes: The Israel-Egypt Agreement on February 24, 1949, the Israel-Lebanon Agreement on March 23, the Israel-Jordan Agreement on April 3, and the Israel-Syrian Agreement on July 20. These are documented in S/1264/Rev. 1, Security Council, Official Records, Fourth Year: Special Supplement No. 3: General Armistice Agreement between Egypt and Israel. Lake Success, December 13, 1949. Special Supplement No. 4: General Armistice Agreement between Lebanon and Israel. Lake Success, April 8, 1949. Special Supplement No. 1: General Armistice Agreement between Jordan and Israel. Lake Success, June 20, 1949, and Special Supplement No. 2: General Armistice Agreement between Syria and Israel. Lake Success, June 20, 1949. Iraq, Saudi Arabia and Yemen, which had also been involved in the invasion of Palestine, refused to sign armistice agreements. The Iraqis, who played a substantial military role in the war, declined to sign on the grounds that they had no common frontier with Israel.

7. For a critical analysis of the process leading to the Sinai and Golan agreements between Israel and Egypt, and Israel and Syria, which followed the 1973 October War, and for verbatim citation of the agreements, see Matti Golan, *The Secret Conversations of Henry Kissinger, Step-by-Step Diplomacy in the Middle East,* translated from the Hebrew by R. and S. Stern. New York: Quadrangle/The New York Times Book Co., 1976, 280 pp.

8. Colin Williams, *Jerusalem: A Universal Cultural and Historical Resource,* an Occasional Paper. New York: Aspen Institute for Humanistic Studies, undated, 17 pp. In this paper, Williams addresses the religious requirements of the three major faiths with a stake in Jerusalem as background to a political future that would retain its three-fold symbolism.

9. Williams, *ibid.,* pp. 9-10. See also Michael Avi-Yonah, "Byzantine Jerusalem," and Eliyahu Ashtor and Haim Hirschberg, "Crusader Period," in *Jerusalem,* Israel Pocket Library, Jerusalem: Keter Publishing Company, 1973, pp. 43-47 and 60-68.

10. Eliahu Ashtor and Haim Hirschberg, "Arab Period," and "Mameluk Period," in *Jerusalem, ibid.,* pp. 48-59, 69-76. See also Yehoshua Ben Arieh, "The Old City of Jerusalem," a paper presented at the Association of American Geographers Meeting, April 1975, pp. 16-21 (mimeo).

11. Guy Le Strange, *History of Jerusalem Under the Moslems,* reprinted from *Palestine Under the Moslems,* Jerusalem: Ariel Publishing Company (no

date), pp. 145-150. The author quotes Mukadassi in the tenth century as saying: "Ramlah is the capital of Palestine. It is a fine city and well built . . . It possesses magnificent hostelries and pleasant baths, dainty foods and various condiments, spacious houses, fine mosques and broad roads . . . It is situated on the plain, and is yet near both to the mountains and the sea."

12. W.D. Davies points out the emphasis upon the land in Judaism, and the centrality of Jerusalem within the broader concept of Israel's centrality. Yet he notes: "Under often harsh realities and vicissitudes, far-flung exile and the blandishment of assimilation, in many a Babylon, the sentiment for the land of Israel has often been tempered, suppressed, and even ignored and rejected by many Jews" (despite its being rooted in the scriptures and nourished in the liturgy). W.D. Davies, *The Gospel and the Land – Early Christianity and Jewish Territorial Doctrine*, Berkeley: University of California Press, 1974, p. 158. Harel's account of the high and low periods of Jewish settlement in Jerusalem from the destruction of the Second Temple (70 A.D.) to the end of Ottoman rule emphasizes the changing salience of pilgrimage and scholarship in Jerusalem to Jews throughout the world in these different periods. Menashe Harel, *Zot Yerushalayim*, (Hebrew), Tel Aviv: Am Oved, 1972, pp. 38-63.

13. Ben Arieh notes that Jerusalem's geographical-religious characteristics find expression in five ways: population, morphology of the city, economy, genre de vie, and spiritual perception. See Yehoshua Ben Arieh, "The Old City of Jerusalem — A Religious City," *op. cit.*, pp. 27-30.

Geopolitical Imperatives: The Case for a Unified Jerusalem

The case for a unified Jerusalem is based upon five geopolitical imperatives, which set the stage for rationalizing Israeli national control of the Holy City, irrespective of whatever internal geopolitical structural changes may take place. The imperatives are as follows:

(1) *The national value that a people attach to territory as a result of bitter struggles that are conducted to assure their ties to this territory, is of the highest order, especially when struggles are carried on with little external assistance.*

(2) *A varied lowland-upland landscape is a basic national geopolitical objective. Jerusalem's city and corridor have links with historic Jewish settlement patterns and are the major focus for Israel's upland development. To fulfill the objective, the upland must be securely tied to the coastal plain.*

(3) *The uniqueness of each part of Jerusalem demands very special responses to the challenge of integrating the city as a system. With the accommodation and compromises that must characterize these responses come greater dependence of the whole on the specialized parts.*

(4) *Jerusalem has extended its strategic and economic reach over the most important parts of Arab Palestine. This makes for a set of*

links between Israel and the heart of the West Bank which will not be easily broken.

(5) *The shift in relative location of Jerusalem from peripheral to focal in Israel, has stimulated the city's growth in unprecedented fashion. With this shift Jerusalem is rapidly becoming a competing political core to the Tel Aviv core within the Jewish state. It is also becoming focal, once again, to much of the Arab West Bank.*

The first four of these imperatives will be treated in this chapter, the fifth in the next one.

A PEOPLE'S STRUGGLE FOR THE LAND

The national value that a people attach to territory as a result of bitter struggles that are conducted to assure their ties to this territory, is of the highest order, especially when struggles are carried on with little external assistance.

Probably no other city in the world has suffered from recurrent warfare as has Jerusalem.[1] We shall not dwell on the wars it may have endured from its founding as the City of Shalem in the third millenium B.C. to its conquest by David from the Jebusites just after the beginning of the 10th century B.C. But from Jerusalem's establishment as David's capital, its endurance through external attack, internal strife and destruction have proved its eternality. Major cataclysmic events have brought blood, fire, devastation and woe to the city (See Table 1).

Table 1
Jerusalem's Catalog of Conflict

1. Destruction by Babylonians (587 or 586 B.C.)
2. Seleucid Conquest (198 B.C.)
3. Capture by Antiochus Epiphanes (170 B.C.)
4. Hasmonean Revolt, Occupation & Defeat, & Reoccupation (164-141 B.C.)
5. Pompey's Siege (63 B.C.)
6. Conquest by Herod (37 B.C.)
7. Destruction by Romans (70 A.D.)
8. Bar Cochba Revolt (132-135 A.D.)
9. Persian Conquest (614 A.D.)

10. Muslim Conquest (638 A.D.)
11. Seljuk Conquest (1071, 1076 A.D.) .
12. Fatmid Conquest (1098 A.D.)
13. First Crusader Siege and Conquest (1099 A.D.)
14. Siege of Saladin (1187 A.D.)
15. Third Crusader Siege (1229 A.D.)
16. Conquest and Sacking by Tartars (1244 A.D.)
17. Starvation relieved by Allenby's Entry (1917 A.D.)
18. Arab Mob Outbreaks in Old City (1920, 1929, 1936-1939 A.D.)
19. Jewish Underground Violence (1944-1946 A.D.)
20. Arab-Jewish Conflict (1947 A.D.)
21. Arab Siege and Conflict (1948 A.D.)
22. Jewish Conquest of East Jerusalem (1967 A.D.)

This catalog of conflict is by no means comprehensive, nor can it be assumed that the list is final, given the unresolved status of the Arab-Israeli struggle. Moreover, in eschatological terms, the ultimate war or catastrophe is yet to come, for the external peace that will follow the ingathering of the exiles comes only after the Day of Judgment in which unworthy nations will be annihilated in the Valley of Yehoshaphat.[2]

Struggles of the Past

The memory that the Jewish people has of its struggle to maintain itself in the territory is long. Nothing in Jerusalem's catalog of conflict so stirs the emotion as a reading of the horror and brutalities of the long, drawn-out Jewish War, especially those that attended the destruction of the Second Temple. In describing this last catastrophe, Josephus writes: "No destruction ever wrought by God or man approached the wholesale carnage of this war. Every man who showed himself was either killed or captured by the Romans, and then those in the sewers were ferreted out . . . and killed. . . . There was no one left for the soldiers to kill or plunder . . . so Caesar now ordered them to raze the whole city."[3] Josephus estimates that 97,000 prisoners were taken and that 1,100,000, mostly Jews, were killed in the siege.[4] That such a catastrophic event left its mark on the Jewish national psyche, a mark even greater than the one left when the King of Babylon had stormed Jerusalem and laid it waste 650 years before, is undeniable. Only the Holocaust that was to take place

1900 years after Jerusalem's destruction was to sear the national psyche in a similar way.

What happened in Jerusalem two millenia ago, while never to be forgotten, does not have the contemporary geopolitical import of what has happened in the past half century, and especially in 1947-1949, in the nineteen years of division that followed and in June, 1967. It is the wars that the past two generations have directly experienced that, above all, fashion contemporary political responses.

To those who make Israel's decisions today, the three days of the Arab pogroms upon Jews caught in the Jewish Quarter of the Old City in the Passover of 1920 begin the memory chain. British troops sealed off the Old City so that Jewish self-defense groups could not enter to provide protection from the Arab mob that was running amok.[5] In 1929 came Arab assaults on the isolated Jewish quarter of the Old City, in Motza, then a distant western suburb, and in Kibbutz Ramat Rahel, then on Jerusalem's southern periphery. Again, when the riots began in 1936, accompanied by a general strike proclaimed by the Arab Higher Committee, Jerusalem was affected. This time, however, Jewish settlements in the hills around Jerusalem were also exposed to Arab attack, provoking in reaction the development of Hagana mobile field forces which took the offensive against the Arabs.[6]

The Modern Struggle — Independence

All of this was prelude to the major struggle for Jerusalem. War began with the Palestine Partition Plan of November 29, 1947, and broke out in full fury upon the establishment of the Jewish State on May 14, 1948. This volume is not a history of Israel's War of Independence or even of the battles for Jerusalem. But certain events and places are crucial to our understanding of the relationship between conflict and territorial attachment.

Three days after the United Nations' Palestine Partition Resolution, Arabs reacted by burning and looting the Jewish Commercial Center in the new city. The conflict within and surrounding the city continued over the next four months. The Arab ring around Jerusalem was closed — with increasing attacks upon the Jerusalem-Tel Aviv Road, especially in the deep, forested valley of Shaar HaGay, the gateway to the Jerusalem Corridor from the coastal plain.[7] The Etzion bloc of four Jewish settlements in the Hebron Hills was cut off from Jerusalem in January, eventually falling to the Arab Legion in May. The siege of the city itself began in February, when the Arabs blew up the road between Shaar HaGay and Kastel (See Figure 5).

Key events in the early stages of the battle for the city included: 1) the unsuccessful attempt to hold the Jewish Quarter of the Old City which was captured by the Arab Legion on May 28 after the War of Independence had broken out; 2) seizure on April 3-4 by Jewish forces of the village of Kastel from Arab irregulars. Kastel, site of an ancient Roman camp and Crusader castle, overlooked the main highway's approaches to Jerusalem's western entrance; 3) massacre by Jewish terrorists on April 8 of the Arab villagers of Deir Yassin, a small village on the western outskirts; 4) destruction by Arab irregulars of a Jewish medical convoy in Sheikh Jarrah bound for Mount Scopus, April 13; 5) occupation of the Katamon Quarter by Jewish forces on April 28; 6) evacuation of Jewish settlement in northern Jerusalem — Atarot and Naveh Yakov, May 14; 7) capture by Israel on May 14, the day of the British evacuation of the British security zones. There were four such cantonments. They had been created in February, 1947, as wired and guarded compounds, controlled by gates, to provide secure residences and work space for the British. Because the zones covered nearly one-third of West Jerusalem and controlled all north-south movement, their speedy capture by Jewish forces meant, in effect, that West Jerusalem was fully in Jewish hands. The cantonments were: Zone C (containing "Bevingrad" — the C.I.D. fortress headquarters, the Russian Compound, General Post Office and Notre Dame); Zone B (King David Hotel, YMCA, King George Street, Talbiah, Terra Sancta); Zone A (German Colony); and Zone D (Schneller Military Barracks).[8]

With the evacuation of the British, the sporadic battles for Jerusalem turned into a continuous, all out struggle until interrupted by the first truce on June 11. The Arab Legion took Sheikh Jarrah on May 14. This cut off Mount Scopus and secured Arab access to the Old City which was entered the next day. In Southern Jerusalem, the Legion fought for Ramat Rahel, but failed to capture it. Israel's principal southern outpost, Ramat Rahel, overlooked traffic on the road between Jerusalem and Bethlehem. Farther south, however, the Legion captured the Etzion bloc settlements so that the city was now open to invasion from the south. Meanwhile the road to Tel Aviv had been completely cut (the last convoy arrived on April 20). Supplies could not be brought in from

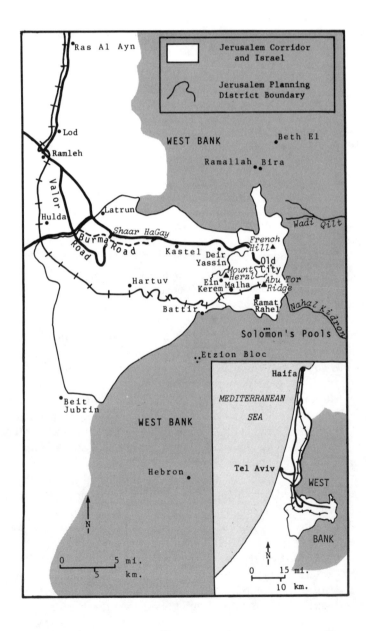

**Fig. 5. The Jerusalem Corridor and Lifelines to Jerusalem —
1948 to Present**

the coastal plain. Also in early May, the Arabs had cut the water pipelines: from Ras al Ayn in the coastal plain foothills, from Solomon's pools near Hebron, and from the Ein Farah springs in the bed of Wadi Qilt east of Jerusalem. The population of Jerusalem faced not only the Arab Jordan Legion attacking from the east and north, Egyptian forces from the south, and Arab irregulars and the Legion in the hills surrounding the Corridor to the west, they also had to contend with starvation and thirst. By the beginning of June, the food ration was down to 900 calories daily per person, and water which starting in January, had been secretly stored in ancient cisterns that had been cleaned, was running out.[9]

Very much a part of the Battle for Jerusalem were the battles for Latrun. Controlled by the Arab Legion, Latrun overlooked the gateway to the Jerusalem Corridor. Three times (May 23, May 30, and June 9-10), Israeli forces attempted to capture the salient and failed. Several hundred Israelis, including many immigrants dispatched from ships directly into battle lines, were killed in the vain attempts to secure Jerusalem.

The truce of June 11 ended the hostilities, giving Jerusalemites a respite after weeks of shelling. When the fighting broke out again on July 9, Lod and Ramleh fell to the Israelis. However, a strategem for capturing Latrun by seizing the Latrun-Ramallah road and cutting off the salient failed. The second truce which started on July 19 put an end to further attempts to dislodge the Legion from Latrun.

Meanwhile in Jerusalem, Ein Kerem and Malha at the western edge of the city and Mount Herzl were captured by Israeli forces. The Arabs in the Old City repulsed efforts by Israeli forces to gain entry, but the Arab Legion was held to a standstill in its attacks in Musrara.

South of the city, counter-attacking Israeli troops tried to seize the entire Abu Tor-Ramat Rahel Ridge from Arabs who had penetrated the demilitarized zone (the northern end of the ridge is called Givat Hananya and the highest point at Government House, Jebel Mukaber). Losses were heavy, and neither side emerged the victor. As part of a strategy to relieve Mount Scopus, an attack was planned on Sheikh Jarrah, the link between the Old City and Scopus. Time ran out before it could be mounted. Had Mount Scopus fallen completely into Israeli hands and been linked to the Jewish sector via French Hill, it would have posed a

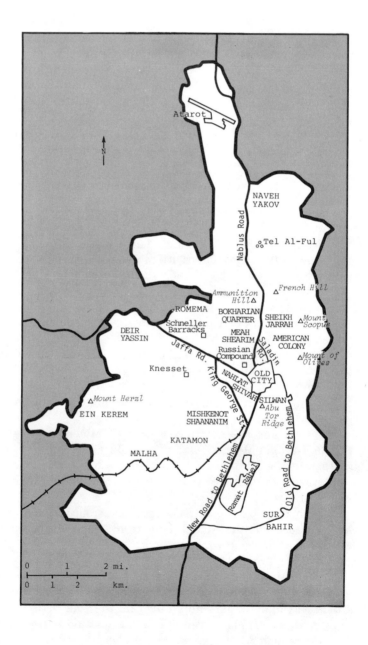

Fig. 6. Jerusalem Reference Map

major problem for the Arabs because of its potential to control the road to Jericho. Instead, surrounded by the Legion, it was to remain a strategic liability for Israel for 19 years, despite some utility as an observation point.

The third round of fighting broke out on October 14. In Jerusalem, major action took place on Mount Zion, commanding the Jewish neighborhood of Yemin Moshe and held by Israelis despite exposure to heavy fire from the walls of the Old City. The most important tactical gains of the fighting were made by the Israelis when they captured all of the approaches to the railroad as it entered the city from the southwest. Equally important, on the eve of the cease-fire on October 22, the Corridor was broadened by victories that cleared the area beyond Bet Shemesh as far as Beit Gubrin and Battir.

Statistics of casualties do not fully describe the impact of the battles for Jerusalem upon Jerusalemites and upon all of Israel. But of approximately 6,000 persons killed during the War of Independence (4,000 soldiers and 2,000 civilians), the struggle for Jerusalem cost the lives of 1,976 persons — one-third of all those killed in the War of Independence. If the casualty figures of the battles for Latrun are added, the struggle for Jerusalem accounted for about half of those Israelis killed. The magnitude of these losses helps explain the intensity of Israeli feeling about the price of securing the Jerusalem foothold. Moreover, the proportion of civilians killed in Jerusalem was much higher than the nation-wide proportion. No wonder Jerusalem's citizens were so highly conscious of their front-line status.

The end of the war brought two decades of relative calm. From 1948 through 1967, incidences of shooting and terrorist attacks across the armistice lines in Jerusalem were frequent, but at a level still acceptable to Israelis. Partition exacted its price, but it was not as heavy a price as that of war. Matters changed abruptly with the outbreak of the Six Day War on June 5, 1967. Despite Israel's formal declaration that if Jordan refrained from entering the conflict Israel would take no warlike steps against her, the Jordanians began hostilities immediately that morning. Mount Scopus and West Jerusalem were shelled with artillery and mortars, and an attack was launched to seize Government House on Jebel Mukaber in the demilitarized zone of the Abu Tor ridge.

The battle for Jerusalem was fierce. In the three days of action between the Arab Legion and Jewish forces, casualties were heavy. King Hussein stated that 6,000 Jordanians were killed or listed missing in action during the Six Day War.[10] Estimate of losses in Jerusalem, were 645, over 400 military casualties and 240 civilians, the latter mostly a result of the shelling of the Old City.[11] Those killed in Jerusalem on the Jewish side numbered 200 (179 soldiers). Since 766 Israeli soldiers died in the Six Day War, Jerusalem's share of over 25% was again disproportionate, as it has been in the War of Independence. The hard fighting at such places as Ammunition Hill, Abu Tor, Sheikh Jarrah, Nablus Road, Saladin Road, Tel al-Ful, Rockefeller Museum and the Bridge to the Lion's Gate, left an indelible memory on the Israeli national consciousness. "They can have all the rest back," said one, "but not our Holy City."[12] This statement made by a soldier to a reporter on the Temple Mount during the final phase of the battle for the Old City probably speaks for most Israelis on the issue of Jerusalem's future.

A clear expression of how people feel about a place are the monuments that they erect, and the names which they give to places. Jerusalem's monuments and place names strongly reflect the emotions of battle and the desire to remember. The ubiquity of these symbols illustrates the concentration of Israeli attention and feeling on that piece of territory known as Jerusalem.

Understanding the Consequences

It is a geopolitical imperative that strong emotional ties to territory are intensified by war. Failure by external powers to recognize its significance is a major shortcoming in their efforts to help find a solution to the Arab-Israeli conflict. An important volume by the former United States Minister-Consul General in Jerusalem, Evan M. Wilson, is offered as a case in point. In *Jerusalem, Key to Peace,* references to the War of Independence are tense and so "balanced" as to distort what actually happened:[13] "In 1948, upon termination of the Mandate for Palestine, the city became the scene of heavy fighting. . . . Because the narrow Jerusalem Corridor, linking the sea to the rest of Israel, and secured after bitter fighting in the 1948 war, was a salient thrusting eastward into Jordanian territory, any extension of the city after 1948 had to take place to the west. . . . When fighting resumed in July . . . they (the Israelis) also secured and held after bitter fighting a corridor to Jerusalem. The city itself was partly occupied by them and partly by the Arabs." With these brief references Wilson disposes of the military engagements, spearheaded on the Arab side by the British-officered and led Arab Legion that had involved siege and incessant bombardment and that ultimately deprived Israelis and Jews everywhere from access to historical holy places revered for three thousand years.

Again, in discussing the June, 1967 War, Wilson writes: "About noon, after firing had broken out in the Jerusalem area . . . the ill-conceived Jordanian entry into the Government House area had two important consequences. Not only did it give the Israeli Army an excuse to seize a valuable tactical advantage but it also severely hampered UNTSO (United Nations Truce Supervision Organization). . . . The residents of the New City spent the entire period of hostilities in their shelters, which accounts for the low figure of only 15 civilians killed (of whom 11 were air-raid wardens)."

Wilson does refer to heavy hand-to-hand combat and to the damage of 1,300 houses in the Israeli sector in the first few hours of shelling. Moreover, he disclaims at the outset his intention of writing another account of the June, 1967 War. However, beyond the factual information presented, there is no evidence of an appreciation of the depth of feeling in Israel about the two wars in Jerusalem that were thrust upon them by Arab attacks.

Another significant volume by a Foreign Service Officer who served in Israel and other Middle Eastern countries, H. Eugene Bovis, is *The Jerusalem Question.*[14] This balanced and sound study of the religious and political problems facing Israel today makes only one reference to the War of Independence: "Despite the efforts of the U.N., Jerusalem was not spared the trials of war. In fact serious fighting had taken place in the city in the spring, as both the Arabs and Jews jockeyed for the best possible position before the end of the mandate. A truce had been arranged for the Walled City on May 2, and was extended to the whole city a week later. However, the truce was shaky at best and collapsed on May 15." The brevity of the reference to what happened in 1947-48 does not convey the Israeli perspective. However, in contrast to many Mid-East observers this perspective was understood by the author, who stated later in the volume: "If there was strong feeling in 1948 that Israel should hold on to that part of Jerusalem won by Jewish blood, the feeling is even stronger today in regard to the whole city. The Jordanian period was one of the few periods in history when the Jews were not allowed to pray at the Wailing Wall."

While the Western world fully appreciates the strength of the geopolitical-historical imperative in parallel situations, it has failed to do so in the case of Israeli attitudes towards Jerusalem. Despite the Cold War, Americans understood and accepted Russian territorial annexation after World War II as a response to the Nazi invasion and their wartime suffering. Without similar understanding and acceptance for Israel's position in the Jerusalem case, there is little hope for future diplomatic and political movement.

UNITY OF LANDSCAPE THROUGH HETEROGENEITY: LINKING LOWLANDS AND UPLANDS

A varied lowland-upland landscape is a basic national geopolitical objective. Jerusalem's city and corridor have links with historic Jewish settlement patterns and are the major focus for Israel's upland development. To fulfill the objective, the upland must be securely tied to the coastal plain.

When Jews "ascend" to the mountain plateau of Jerusalem that averages 750 meters above sea level (lowest points are 600 meters and highest points are 835 meters), a variety of images are evoked. Some of these are religious, some historic-cultural and some physical-environmental. Recent military events suggest that the "ascent" to Jerusalem is now far more than a matter of symbolism; it is an ascent to a modern-day fortress region that safeguards much of the rest of the country. The steeply-twisting modernized highway route is the link between Israel, the coastal plain enclave, and the Israel of the mountains (See Figure 5). It is 25 kilometers in length from its start at the head of Emek Ayyalon (Shaar HaGay) to the entrance to Jerusalem.

Mountainous Palestine (Samaria, Judea, the Galilee) was the homeland of the ancient Jews. At that time Jerusalem was close to the junction of upland highways. Its site was just east of the crest of hills that are the spine of the mountains of Judea and Samaria, and situated atop a mountain saddle 200 meters lower than the mountains of Beth El to the north, and of Hebron to the south. The north-south trunk road connected Beersheba with Schechem (Nablus) and Ginai (Jenin); the east-west road (running north of Jerusalem) tied Jaffa to Jericho and Rabat Ammon (Amman).[15] There were competitors perhaps more favorably sited for this crossroads function. These included Givon (Jib), eight kilometers to the northwest, and Beth El (Beitin), 15 kilometers to the north. These towns lay astride the east-west route from the coastal plain via Emek Ayyalon to the Jordan via Wadi Qilt. But once the City of David acquired its religious significance, it was able to maintain its primacy down through the ages.[16] From its high accessibility site, fortified on three sides by deep valleys and favored with an assured water supply, Jerusalem could dominate all of Judea, and was in a strong position to extend its influence throughout eastern Samaria. Jerusalem became in fact as well as in name the capital, the city up to which all Jews had an obligation to ascend.[17]

Zionist Return to the Lowland

The modern Jewish return to Palestine, starting in 1881-82 and continuing beyond independence, took place on the plains and not in the traditional mountain homeland. This is an irony of history. The plains in Israelite times had been inhabited by others, Philistia (from Jaffa to Gaza) and the northern coast (from Acre to Tyre) not even being part of the Kingdom of Israel. But the plains were essentially empty when the Zionist return began. The coast, on occasions settled by Jews during their history of pre-modern settlement, and long since abandoned by Philistines, Phoenicians, Romans, Greeks and Crusaders had, with the coming of the Ottomans, fallen into decline and disuse. The Palestinian native stock, now largely Arab, remained or became an upland village peasantry. Many of the Arabs whom modern Jewish settlers did encounter on the coast were of nineteenth century immigrant stock, especially Egyptian. They had been attracted by railroad building and urbanization processes initiated by Europeans under the Ottoman rule. With the onset of the British Mandate after World War I and with heightened economic activities by Jews and the Mandatory Government, conditions became even more favorable for immigration of non-indigenous Arabs into the coastal areas. By 1948-49, therefore, relatively few of the Arabs with whom Jewish settlers interacted on the coastal plain were of native stock.

Jerusalem — The Major Upland Center

During the pre-statehood period of modern Jewish settlement, Jerusalem was the major upland area to attract large-scale Jewish immigration. The new immigration augmented the pre-existing Jewish population base that had been built up there during the Ottoman period. Jewish settlement had retained a foothold in upland areas for the four hundred years of Turkish rule. The holy cities of Safed and Tiberias in the Galilee outstripped Jerusalem's Jewish community in size from the 16th to the 18th centuries, but Jerusalem reemerged as the largest Jewish center of settlement at the beginning of the nineteenth century. Indeed, so pre-eminent was Jerusalem for Jews that until World War I, more than half of all the Jews of Palestine continued to live there.

As residents of the only town in Palestine to have uninterrupted Jewish settlement (even during the ban of the late Crusader period), Jews were the dominant population for much of Jerusalem's history. They were the single largest group throughout most of the nineteenth century, consisting of 55% or more of the population for the last three quarters of a century. In 1896, the proportion of Jews to the total population was 62%; the corresponding figures for 1913, 1948, 1967 and 1975 were 64%, 61%, 74% and 73%.

Neither Zionist settlement nor an independent Israel was physically restricted to the Coastal Plain. The interior valleys, Jezreel, Upper Jordan, the Arava, and the uplands of the Galilee and Negev were also part of the new state's territory. But rural Upland Galilee was already largely populated by Arabs who had remained after the establishment of the state. Moreover, the mountainous section of the Negev could support almost no population. After 1948-49, then, Jerusalem and its Corridor, astride the routes to Samaria, Judea and the Jordan Valley, provided the major focus for new upland settlement. Jerusalem was thus the major focus for developing a more varied national landscape.

CHALLENGE OF INTEGRATING THE CITY AS A SYSTEM

The uniqueness of each part of Jerusalem demands very special responses to the challenge of integrating the city as a system.

With the accommodation and compromises that must characterize these responses come greater dependence of the whole on the specialized parts.

What are the implications for Jerusalem of the population and physical growth that it has experienced with reunification? For those who live in this urbanized upland, the environmental advantages are many: the natural beauty of Judea's mountains, trees, water and, to the east, desert; the brisk climate of sunny but cool summers and mild winters; forests for recreation; availability of building stone; amenities of national and international educational and cultural institutions; an ambience that is a unique blending of past and present. Jerusalem's planners have profited from the negative experiences of the large-scale, unplanned growth of the cities of Israel's Center, especially Tel Aviv. In Jerusalem physical and social planning is well advance. This is not to gloss over the fact that the hectic building pace that has been generated out of security and political considerations, has on more than a few occasions permitted unaesthetic or poorly located development, or has rationalized economic gain from excessively high-rise structures.[18]

Problems of Growth

Major problems attend the city's growth and serve as challenges to its development as a system. Unification of the city in 1967 was accompanied by an outward extension of Jerusalem's boundaries to the north, south and east, into areas of both urban and rural Arab settlement.[19] Unified Jerusalem now includes ten former independent Arab municipalities and West Jerusalem. With an area of 104 square kilometers, it is more than three times as large as was the Jerusalem of 1947 (30 square kilometers).

In the expanded city, large-scale, clustered apartment building has taken place to create new Jewish anchor points or bases on the eastern side of the city. In the first stage of recent growth, the Mount Scopus enclave was linked to Jewish Jerusalem by the construction of several thousand housing units to the west, in Ramat Eshkol, in Givat HaMivtar and, to the north, in Givat Shapira (Givah Zarfatit). Most recently, four large-scale developments have been sited at the city's new outer boundaries: north, adjoining the road to Ramallah and Nablus at Naveh Yakov; northwest at Ramot (Navi Samuil); south, off the road to Bethlehem, at Armon HaNatziv looking eastward to the Judean desert; and at Giloh looking southwest to Beit Jalah. The massive apartment housing estates are designed on a sufficiently large-scale to provide the security of the majority (See Figure 7).

These residential areas are peripheral developments and if they are to be fully integrated with the core of the city, there will have to be radical changes in that core (e.g., creating a new transportation system to serve the center, adequate parking facilities, expanded commercial and other services). One option is to have the outlying housing estates develop independent service and employment structures. Such a development would mean loss of the efficiencies and amenities of a city's center, and the weakening of the quality of integrated city life. Jerusalem will have to choose: will these outlying northern and southern suburbs, and the western ones built in the 1950s and early 1960s become isolated and semi-independent, as so often has occurred in American metropolitan growth, or will they be integrated in form and function with the central portions of the city.

Other problems that came with growth include: lack of integration between the Old Walled City and the modern Jewish Commercial core in the Western Jerusalem sector that expands from Zion Square and thus away from the Walled City; the centripetal forces affecting university life, with the building of two separate major Hebrew University campuses (at Givat Ram and at Mount Scopus); the pressures to concentrate national government functions in one major area within the western basin in the new city; and the competition for space between commercial and residential areas on the one hand, and the industrial areas on the other.

Above all, there is the problem of how to maintain the quality of life of what was not so long ago a small city, in the face of continued pressures for growth.[20] When does a city reach the point that its residents lose touch with the leadership and with one another? Some key benchmarks are when people become overwhelmed by the noise and fumes of traffic; when the individuality of neighborhoods is overpowered by the mass of the city; when population crowding and loss of open spaces become oppressive to the individual. While there is no precise population ceiling which, if exceeded, would rob Jerusalem of its unique qualities, there are certain density danger points that must be carefully monitored if Jerusalem is to remain Jerusalem. Those guiding Jerusalem's growth must answer to future as well as present generations, to Muslims and Christians as well as to Jews.

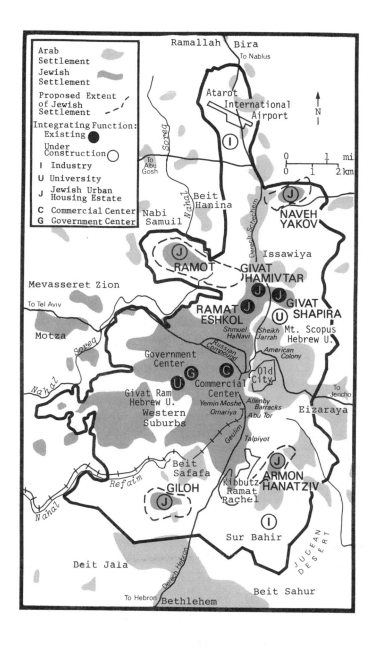

Fig. 7. Israeli Developments in East Jerusalem

A major issue facing Jerusalem in terms of optimal size of population is relationship to spatial capacity. At the end of 1975, population had reached 356,000; by 1992, it is expected to reach over half a million residents. Just prior to reunification, the East and West Jerusalem municipalities combined had a population of 240,000 in an area of 30 square kilometers. Population density was therefore 8,000 persons per square kilometer. Today, Jerusalem has a population density of 3,500 persons per square kilometer in 104 square kilometers. Statistically, the unified city is 50% less crowded than was pre-1967 Jerusalem. But the cost of lowering the density is a more dispersed city, requiring proportionately higher infrastructural costs, especially utilities and transportation. The real question in assessing these costs is whether the dispersal is being accomplished by spread of housing over much of the area (creating a horizontal urban profile), or whether the housing is being concentrated in a few very dense subcenters (creating an interrupted vertical urban profile). Lower population density for the city masks the clustering of high rise apartment buildings in several of the newer neighborhoods, especially those of East Jerusalem. Apartment houses appeared in their modern form in Jerusalem in the 1930s; from the early 1950s to the present, they have become the major form of Jewish settlement in Jerusalem.

Clustered Living

Reasons for the development of the high density pockets are not only economic in that they attempt to reduce some of the costs of dispersal, but they also fulfill cultural, environmental and security needs. From a cultural standpoint, the modern apartment house has been a fixture of the Israeli residential landscape since the 1920s especially Tel Aviv. Clustered living for the Jews of Israel has its roots in the urban blocks of Eastern Europe as well as the more contemporary urban Mediterranean scene. In Jerusalem, lack of flat land has made buildable land a more scarce commodity. High land rents, therefore, cause intensified use of hill top and upper slopes.

The security issue is not a new factor in Jerusalem's residential building strategy. Physical security needs kept the population within the walls of the Old City up to a century and a quarter ago. But even within the Old City, communities that lived separately sought security from one another by building separate physical compounds. Old Jerusalem was a city of "walls within walls," the Armenian Quarter being a particularly good example of a physically-secure neighborhood with inner court yards used for communal purposes. When settlement extended outside the Old City, the need for security increased. Well into the nineteenth century, the Sanjak of Jerusalem was a powerless administrative entity. While people within the city's massive walls were safe when the gates clanged shut at night, outside the case was different. Marauding Bedouins attracted by the upland Judean pastures roamed the area with their sheep and goats. They terrorized surrounding farm communities and even towns like Jericho and Bethlehem. Moreover, they controlled the routes into Jerusalem from the west (via Ramleh) and from the east (via Jericho).

When settlement expanded outside the Old City walls, protection was often sought through compounds — long, connected one-to-two-storied row buildings with internal courtyards and the houses themselves serving as exterior walls. The first Jewish quarters (Mishkenot Shaananim, 1856-60; Nahlat Shivah, 1869; Meah Shearim, 1873) were examples of this form of security settlement. Windows and doors of the individual units faced inward to the courtyard, with its well communal kitchen, etc. Meah Shearim is the best preserved of what was built as a kind of collective apartment block. A late nineteenth century type of layout offering security with family privacy was the Bokharian Quarter — separate apartment houses built around courtyards. From the turn of the century into the 1930s, concern for physical safeguard against Arab rioting continued to be an important reason for clustering.[21]

After the War of Independence, long, reinforced attached concrete apartment blocks were constructed by Israel along the Jordanian border of the city in Shemuel HaNavi and the Katamonim. This continued the process of building quarters so as to provide residents with maximum physical security. The tradition continues today, in the construction and layout of the massive, fortress-like apartment developments built by Israelis in the housing estates of East Jerusalem.

Jerusalem's "security complex" has not been restricted to Jewish settlement. Early Christian settlements outside the wall also took compound form. The first and most impressive undertaking was the Russian Compound. Built from 1860-64, it adjoined the northwest corner of the Old City. The compound included hostels, a cathedral and a hospital to serve the thousands of Russians (estimated at 12,000 in 1866) who were the dominant group of pilgrims to visit Jerusalem. In his volume published in 1880, Charles Wilson describes the Russian Compound in these terms: "Without the walls (of the Old City) towards the northwest is the great Russian establishment, consulate, cathedral, and hospice which, like some great fortress or barrack, overshadows and completely dominates the Holy City."[22] A German orphanage and school, later named the Schneller Barracks after its founder, and the small settlement of the American colony established in 1881 were much smaller-scale versions of the Russian Compound. When in 1947-48, at the height of both Jewish and Arab resistance to British rule, the Mandatory Government moved all British troops and civil servants into security zones protected by barbed wire fences, it was following the time-honored Jerusalem tradition of seeking security behind walls.

British and Israeli Planning Policies

Amidst all of the social, political, economic and cultural forces that contribute to the planning and development of Jerusalem, there is one force, often in contradiction with some of the others, that has maintained itself with consistency. This is the effort by Jerusalem's leadership of the past half century to have the New City's buildings and general infrastructure conform to the physical setting. Thus, it is required by law that all buildings be made of Jerusalem stone, a warm, mellow pinkish-white or rose-colored Turonian limestone.[23] Also, there is special concern for maintaining lines of sight and for safeguarding the unbroken lines of landscape contours. The British were especially careful to limit buildings in both absolute height and relative height (related to the skyline of the ridge). Legislatively, these concerns were expressed through building codes enacted in the McLean Plan (1918) and the Holliday Plan (1930), the latter clearly promoting maintenance of a continuous skyline. The Kendall Plan (1944) took a strong position in trying to spread the built up area by reducing building heights. Happily for Jerusalem today, all British plans were most attentive to preserving open space and to developing green belts.[24]

The Mandatory Government pursued the policy of maintaining Jerusalem as a medium-sized, though modernized and accessible provincial capital town. British authorities and planners were strongly opposed to industrialization, and based the city's employment future on government, tourism, education and commerce. For the State of Israel, such a policy was in conflict with the geopolitical and spiritual need for urban growth. The problem of accommodating aesthetic and economic principles to growth needs, then, became the crucial planning problem. The city was to grow from its (then) western basin core, containing the Jewish commercial center, with residential suburbs as built-up islands separated by wooded valleys. In particular, the Shaviv Plan (1955-59) offered the strategy that while the older parts of West Jerusalem would be a continuous built-up area, the newer (western parts) would be discontiguous, the residences riding the ridges and upper slopes. The farther away from the Old City (the eastern basin), the less concern there was in practice with building heights, partly on the assumption that distance and uneven topography would not permit a level skyline anyway.

Major new problems have arisen since 1967, as the unified city has ceased to spread to the west and developments have turned to the east — in the center, north and south. Emphasis on the western (now central) basin as the core has created pressures there for multi-story buildings — commercial (e.g., the 17-story Plaza Hotel on the crest of Keren Kayemeth Street — the first ridge west of the Old City); residential (the high rise Kiryat Wolfsohn apartment complex that overlooked the Knesset); and governmental (there have been proposals for 25-story towers for the national government complex in the heart of the Western basin).

Negative reaction to such high rise building has resulted in considerable scaling-down of the sudden vertical explosion of the city. Citizens groups and outside specialists (e.g., the Jerusalem Committee first appointed in 1970 by the city to evaluate its planning efforts), had a hand in slowing down the dramatic alteration of the skyline. Their efforts prodded and supported city officials in pressing for more human-scale building, using restrictive building codes in applicable situations, or in opposing national government architectural decisions where possible. Freeway plans that would have destroyed historic neighborhoods in the interests of providing access to and through the western basin, especially the capital area and the adjoining commercial district, have been modified considerably. Still the contradiction between growth and preservation continues. If the contradiction is to be resolved through greater spread or horizontality, then the cost will continue to be high, especially as it relates to the problem of connecting the different neighborhoods and peoples of Jerusalem.

A Heterogeneous City

Dov Joseph, in describing Jerusalem up to 1930, spoke of it as a "mosaic of distinct communities, each living in proud dissociation from its fellows."[25] The city that Joseph described as the Three Jerusalems (the Old City; the Commercial and Education core of West and East Jerusalem outside the walls; and the Ring of relatively close-in suburbs) was a small city. During the British Mandate, separateness was essentially a cultural function because different groups living in close quarters next to each other *chose* to remain different. Today cultural divisions are reinforced by distance and physical barriers, that is, by geographical spread.

Certainly much of what makes Jerusalem unique is that it is heterogeneous — a city of minorities, both of Jews and non-Jews. For Jews there are the observant (ultra-orthadox and orthodox) and the non-observant; the Ashkenazi and the Sepharadi; the Anglo-Saxons, the Germans and the East Europeans; the Yemenites, the Bokharians, the Kurds, the Iraqis and the Moroccans; the intellectuals and the workers. For the non-Jews, there are the Christians — Armenians, Greeks, Western Europeans, Ethiopians and Russians; and the Muslims — urbanites, rural villagers and Bedouins, the Old City dwellers and the East Jerusalem suburbanites, the prosperous merchants and professionals, and the peddlars and street cleaners. How to maintain the richness of this ethnic and religious tapestry is an unparalleled challenge, considering not only the normal social and economic tensions that characterize such a mixed urban area, and the international political pressures that work to divide the Jerusalem scene, but also the clear minority status into which non-Jews have been cast. On the other hand, keen awareness of these problems, accentuated by the fact that "the entire world is looking on," creates a challenge-response situation that appears to be bringing about a faster development of this diversified city as an integrated system, than would otherwise be the case for so fragmented a culture world.

ORGANIC DEVELOPMENT AND OUTREACH

Jerusalem has extended its strategic and economic reach over the most important parts of Arab Palestine. This makes for a set of links between Israel and the heart of the West Bank which will not be easily broken.

Unification of Jerusalem has been accomplished, not merely by the political fiat that was promulgated by Israel after the Six Day War, but by actions that have promoted movement and settlement throughout the boundaries of the city and across its borders. The fundamental character of a Jerusalem controlled by Israel and open to Jewish development is a geopolitical fact that has emerged from a comprehensive Israeli strategy for growth and development of the capital. Not only do these activities make their impact upon the municipal character, they also have strong impact upon the region, and are creating the seeds of a capital region.

The creation of the physical and geopolitical "facts" of an Israeli presence within East Jerusalem has been a consistent policy of the Israeli government, even if subject to considerable internal debate as to its tactical directions. The advice of David Ben Gurion to a number of cabinet ministers in June, 1967, was: "Jews must be brought to East Jerusalem at all costs. Tens of thousands must be settled in a very short time. Jews will agree to settle in East Jerusalem even in huts. One shouldn't wait for the building of regular neighborhoods. The importance is that there should be Jews there."[26] Prime Minister Eshkol took the lead and responsibility for developing this Jewish presence.

The general strategy of the unfolding Israeli development has been: 1) to link East and West Jerusalem by building on and around Mount Scopus in the north and the Abu Tor ridge on the south; 2) to recreate the Jewish Quarter in the Old City (powerful religious and nationalist circles sought to settle Jews throughout the walled city, but were unsuccessful in having such a policy adopted); 3) to build in the northernmost and southernmost sectors of the new boundaries.

The case for building quickly even if it meant temporary facilities was countered by the argument that a permanent Jewish presence must depend upon well-planned, permanent housing. Thus, Ben Gurion's call for temporary housing went unheeded, save for 250 prefabricated student huts that were put up in Mount Scopus in the summer of 1968. The pressure for rapid building did, however, reduce the lead-time desired by planners.

Three land expropriation acts were promulgated in connection with the construction in East Jerusalem:[27] in January, 1968, 3,345 dunams centering around French Hill (Givah Zarfatit) and, Givat HaMivtar; in April, 1968, 881 dunams, mostly in Naveh Yakov, but also the Jewish Quarter of the Old City; in August, 1970, 12,280 dunams — in the Abu Tor ridge (Armon HaNatziv), Sharafat (adjoining Beit Safafa), Nabi Samuil, Atarot, an extension in Naveh Yakov, and the Jewish neighborhood of Shamah (between Mount Zion and Abu Tor), (See Figure 7). Arab and international opposition was especially vocal with news of the first land-taking, when the Arab states protested to the Security Council and were successful in obtaining a resolution denouncing the action.

It may be argued that much of the Israeli activity in East Jerusalem is a return to sites once the focus of Jewish settlement, and not de novo development. In the north, as early as 1920, Jewish laborers established a base at Atarot, adjoining the village (and later airport) of Kalandia. In 1924 a farm settlement (Kfar Ivri) was initiated at Naveh Yakov. These two Jewish centers endured harassment during the next two decades. In April, 1948, the Hagana mounted an operation to secure the settlements by establishing control of Mount Nabi Samuil. The operation failed and the two villages had to be evacuated under fire on the eve and day of independence.

In the south, the Gdud Avoda (Legion of Labor) workers who set up a base camp in Jerusalem in 1923, established the kibbutz of Ramat Rahel in 1926 on the Abu Tor ridge. This settlement held out against continuing Arab attacks during the War of Independence, the armistice placing it adjacent to the Government House (Armon HaNatziv) demilitarized zone.

These three former Jewish areas, as well as Mount Scopus and the Jewish Quarter of the walled city are now major foci for residential, public institutional and industrial activities.

Israeli Development of East Jerusalem

The pace of Israeli construction in East Jerusalem has been exceedingly rapid. By 1973 three major Jewish residential quarters had been completed in the East Center (Ramat Eshkol, Givat

HaMivtar, Givat Shapira). The Jewish Quarter in the Old City and the Hebrew University at Mount Scopus are well on their way to completion. Four outlying housing estates are in various stages of development. Navei Yakov in·the northeast is nearly finished, and Ramot (northwest), Giloh (southwest) and Armon HaNatziv (southeast) are in final stages of first phase development. Already these Israeli housing estates contain half as many residents as the total number of Arabs in East Jerusalem. There are 80,000 Arabs in the newer suburbs and villages of the New City, and about 20,000 in the Old City. Moreover, the total number of projected Israeli housing units is 30,000. As part of a 1980 national housing plan for Jerusalem to accommodate another 100,000 Jews, Giloh and Ramot each have proposed populations of 25,000 to 30,000 for their final building stages!

In the north the new residential estates of Ramot and Naveh Yakov, and the rebuilt international Atarot airport overlook Christian Ramallah and its Muslim twin town Bira. They extend to within three to five kilometers of these Arab centers and thereby dominate all the Beth El Mountains region. From this point the Israeli presence has easy reach to Nablus, the center and main city of eastern Samaria. The Ramot development commands a number of Arab villages northwest of Jerusalem, such as Beit Hanina, Beit Iksa, Nabi Samuil and Givon, and adjoins the height of Har Shmuel (Nabi Samuil). The latter, the highest mountain in Jerusalem's hills (875 meters), overlooks both the Mediterranean and the Dead Seas. Nabi Samuil commands an ancient ridge road that presents an alternative route through the West Bank via Givon to the coastal plain at Latrun. The new development also adjoins a Jerusalem by-pass route that leads southwestward to the Tel Aviv-Jerusalem highway via Abu Gosh. Naveh Yakov controls a by-pass route to the Jordan Valley northeast of Jerusalem, past Anata to the Jericho road. In this area, too, the Anatot industrial zone has been set aside for development as a mixed industrial-trucking center. One center has been built west of Anata and one is proposed northeast of the village. A most powerful expression of the Israeli presence in this area is the military headquarters of the Israeli army central command. Moreover, National Police Headquarters has been relocated from Tel Aviv to Givat HaMivtar.

To the south, the new Israeli suburbs dominate Bethlehem and the Hebron Mountains region, and thus the rest of Judea. The southeastern development of Armon HaNatziv overlooks the major Arab villages east of Jerusalem (Abu Dis, Sur Bahir and Arab Es-Sawakhra), and dominates the eastern suburbs of Bethlehem. The southwestern development of Giloh is on the municipal boundary of Bethlehem and adjoins Beit Jala, the latter a commanding height from which Jordanian artillery once were trained on Jerusalem. Giloh dominates Arab Beit Safafa, immediately to its north. In combination, these two developments serve as modern urbanized counterparts to the neighboring Beit Jala-Bethlehem-Beit Sahur district. Only 25 kilometers from Hebron, they readily extend Jerusalem's reach to this center of Arab Judea.

These northern and southern suburban outgrowths of Jerusalem are major projections which impose the Israeli presence on the key Arab urban centers of Judea and Samaria. They are bases from which transportation routes are being projected that will lead to the widening of the Jerusalem Corridor — not only the Givon-Latrun route that has been discussed, but also a proposed road northwest from Ramallah to Rosh HaAyin and one that will lead southwest from Jerusalem past the Etzion bloc to Beit Jibrin and then Kiryat Gat. They also serve as "hinges" to Jewish agricultural settlements in Judea (Gush Etzion), to the Jewish urban quarter of Hebron, Kiryat Arba, and, potentially, to some of the settlements in the Jordan Valley. Finally, the four developments which lie along the north-south axis of the Mediterranean-Jordan Valley water divide are located at sites that command deeply incised valleys that are part of the rim of the Jerusalem plateau.

Ramot is at the head of the southwestward-flowing Nahal Soreq, and Giloh is at the head of the northwestward-flowing Nahal Refraim. The latter stream joins the former which, fed by another major stream (Nahal Quesalon), flows westward to the Mediterranean south of Tel Aviv. On the slopes of this drainage basin are situated the major highway and railroad to the coast, the latter following the valley of Nahal Refraim from its entrance into Jerusalem. Naveh Yakov is at the head of the eastward-flowing Wadi Farah that becomes Wadi Qilt and flows into the Jordan River at Jericho, and Armon HaNatziv overlooks the southeastward flowing Nahal Kidron. This stream cuts through Judean Desert Bedouin lands on its route to the Dead Sea. The four drainage basins cut by these water courses form a diamond-shaped protective moat (open on the east central side) around Jerusalem.

To complete the circle of the Jerusalem outreach, a major Israeli development has been planned east of the city. This is the
industrial estate to be built at Maale Adummim, 13 kilometers
east of Jerusalem's city limit. Maale Adummim is midway between Jerusalem and the Jericho/Dead Sea area. Projected as a
major site for Jerusalem's industrial expansion, Maale Adummim overlooks the drainage basin of Wadi Qilt. Current proposals are for Jewish residential settlement near the site and a
mixed Arab-Jewish labor pool. Even though Maale Adummim is
not within Jerusalem's corporate limits, the decision of the Israeli
government to build there reflects a firm commitment to the economic development of Jerusalem as a region, with links to West
Bankers as well as Israelis. Ultimately, this industrial development may become the eastern terminus of a major
circumferential highway linking the main Tel Aviv-Jerusalem
road to the Jericho road via the northern part of the city near
Ramot. When completed, Maale Adummim's development will
represent a major strategic as well as economic Israeli presence,
since it lies astride the road to the Jordan Valley.

Strategic Impact on the West Bank

Fulfillment of all of Jerusalem's growth plans will have a
greater strategic impact on the West Bank than small-scale, scattered Jewish agricultural settlements, be they near Hebron, in the
Bika (Jordan Valley) or, as desired by some Israelis, in the heart
of Samaria, near Nablus. Strategically, Arab Samaria and Arab
Judea are now cut off from each other by Jerusalem, and access to
the Bika is controlled from Jerusalem. But this growth needs to
be seen in economic-cultural, as well as strategic terms. Jerusalem is rapidly becoming the modern, primary center for the
most populous part of the West Bank — from Nablus to Hebron to
Jericho. Economic development of Jerusalem means employment,
daily commerce and a broad variety of services for the Arabs of
the West Bank.

Growth of the capital city's labor force since 1967 has been
rapid, with especially positive economic impact upon the Arabs of
East Jerusalem and the West Bank. Jerusalem's total increase
was from 65,000 workers in 1967, to just over 100,000 in 1975.[28]
The Arab labor force jumped from 13.9% in 1968 to 18.6% in 1975.
This includes day laborers from the West Bank. Approximately
10,000 West Bankers, both skilled and semi-skilled, hold jobs in

Jerusalem.[29] About three-quarters of these day laborers are in construction, one-fifth in industry and five percent in services.[30]

The occupational profile of Arabs working in Jerusalem (both of East Jerusalem and the West Bank) differs substantially from that of Jews. Proportionally more Arabs work in industry, trade and building, and significantly less proportionally are engaged in public service and finance. A slightly larger proportion of Arabs are employed in personal services and transportation than are Jews. Many jobs for Arabs in trade, workshops and hotels are generated by tourism, and by the service role of Arab shops to rural Arab villages in the metropolitan area. In general, tourism and small businesses, combined with construction and industrial jobs for Arabs in Jewish sectors of the city, have helped develop a vital, pulsating Arab economy.

The significance of West Bankers for the construction industry, and of construction to the West Bankers is considerable. From 1967 to 1975, over 15,000 residential units (representing about three-quarters of all building footage) have been finished in Jerusalem. This sector above all has stabilized employment for the Arabs. With stable employment have come higher wages, higher living standards and higher social benefits. Arab earnings from jobs in the Israeli economic sector tend to flow back into the Arab sector, to the shops of East Jerusalem, or to improvements in West Bank villages — in housing, transportation, village infrastructure and agriculture.

All of this economic activity can serve as a base, if not a guarantor, for the development of other forms of interaction — social, cultural and political. Surely such economic interaction has a greater possibility for bringing Arabs and Jews closer than single-dimensional schemes of political federalism, or rural settlements by both peoples that are located side-by-side, but that have little interaction.

Today's realities are such that by organic developments within and bordering Jerusalem, Israel has extended its strategic and economic reach over the most important parts of Arab Palestine, making for a set of links between Israel and the heart of the West Bank which are not to be easily broken. Now a Judean upland, as well as a coastal state, Israel has become integrated with the Arab Palestine upland, by becoming physically interconnected with it. Such a physical interconnection was probably not anticipated by proponents of the original approved United Nations

Partition Plan, or by many who espoused a bi-national state. These schemes were predictated on two separate peoples living in two separate parts of Palestine.

Should the Palestine Arabs continue to refuse to seek a political accommodation with Israel, a unified Jerusalem city-region means strategic inferiority for them, without major compensating benefits. Should the Palestinian Arabs choose the path of political cooperation, however, this strategic element will one day lose its overriding significance. For at such a time, the fruits of economic unity and socio-cultural interrelationship will acquire greater importance. This turn of events could bring Arabs and Jews into new and unforeseen dimensions of bi-national coexistence. It is in this context that the growth and development of a unified Jerusalem ought to be viewed — not as a hindrance to peace, but as a major element in the process of interaction that can stimulate the desire for peace.

FOOTNOTES

1. Talmon observes: "Despite the equating of Shalem (a local deity) with "Shalom" (peace) . . . In actual history Jerusalem seldom ceased from being a city of bloodshed and war". Shemaryahu Talmon, "The Biblical Concept of Jerusalem," in *Jerusalem,* edited by John Oesterreicher and Anne Sinai, New York: The John Day Co., 1974, p. 194.

2. Talmon, *ibid.,* p. 202. The author cites *Joel* 4:1f, for the vision of the era of eternal peace to be inaugurated in Jerusalem after tumultuous wars, fought out against the nations, whom God decreed to be annihilated in the valley of Jehoshafat, the valley of His judgement.

3. Josephus, *The Jewish War,* translated from the Latin by G.A. Williamson, London: Penguin, 1959, pp. 338-339.

4. Josephus stressed that the majority of the Jews were not citizens of Jerusalem but had come to the city for Passover and had been caught up in the war. Lieber cites Joachim Jeremias' estimate that the permanent population of Jerusalem at this time probably was not more than 25,000 to 30,000 (See Alfred Lieber, "An Economic History of Jerusalem," in *Jerusalem,* edited by Oesterreicher and Sinai, *op. cit.,* p. 32). Harel proposes the considerably larger figure of 200,000 for this period (See Harel, *Zot Yerushalayim, op. cit.,* p. 64).

5. Meinertzhagen wrote: "I consider these events an exact replica in miniature of a pogrom." He also quotes Hajj al Amin Husseini's message to the Muslims of Hebron: "We are proud of our great victory and of the murder of Jews whom we have killed and the booty we have taken. Do your best through the Chief Secretary (Lt. Col. Waters-Taylor) to assure that the government does not oppose us." See Col. Richard Meinertzhagen, *Middle East Diary, 1917-1956, op. cit.,* pp. 80-84.

6. Yigal Allon, *Shield of David,* Jerusalem: Weidenfeld and Nicolson, 1970, pp. 86-88. Allon describes how Yitshaq Sadeh organized the Hagana's first full-fledged mobile patrol of seventy men, which took the battle to the Arab villages at night.

7. For a succinct description and penetrating analysis of the military events affecting Jerusalem, as well as the entire War of Independence, see Netanel Lorch, *The Edge of the Sword: Israel's War of Independence, 1947-49,* New York: G.P. Putnam's Sons, 1961, 475 pp.

8. For a map of the British Security Zones and supporting British descriptive documentation, see Norman Gosenfeld, *The Spatial Division of Jerusalem, 1948-1969,* University of California, Los Angeles, unpublished Ph.D. dissertation 1973, pp. 28-36.

9. Dov Joseph, *The Faithful City – The Siege of Jerusalem, 1948,* New York: Simon and Schuster, 1960, pp. 147-152.

10. Hussein of Jordan: *My "War" with Israel,* as told to Vick Vance and Pierre Louer, translated from the French by J.P. Wilson and W.B. Michaels, New York: William Morrow & Co., Inc., 1969, p. 88.

11. Benvenisti cites the number of Arabs killed as 645, of whom about 400 were soldiers and 240 were civilians. This is based on those buried by the Municipality of Jerusalem or brought by the Muslim Wakf for reburial from temporary graves. See Meron Benvenisti, *Mul HaHoma HaSegura,* (Hebrew), Jerusalem: Weidenfeld and Nicolson, 1973, p. 119.

12. Abraham Rabinovich, *The Battle for Jerusalem, June 5-7, 1967,* Philadelphia: The Jewish Publication Society of America, 1972, p. 459.

13. Evan M. Wilson, *Jerusalem, Key to Peace,* Washington, D.C.: The Middle East Institute, 1970, pp. 15, 23, 69, 86-88, 100.

14. H. Eugene Bovis, *The Jerusalem Question, 1917-1968,* Stanford: Hoover Institution Press, Stanford University, 1971, pp. 58, 119.

15. Harel suggests that the northern road from Jerusalem via Maalo Adummim and Wadi Qilt to Jericho is an older one than the road known as "Salt Highway" which extended from the northern end of the Dead Sea to Jerusalem via Nabi Musa. See Menashe Harel, "Masaei David V'HaRomaim B'Maale Adummim," (Hebrew), Nispach L'Hakarat HaAretz, *Maarachot 250,* 1976.

16. Yehoshua Ben Arieh, "The Old City of Jerusalem — A Religious City", *op. cit.,* pp. 4-8.

17. Vilnai cites the significance of Jerusalem's mountainous situation and especially Mount Moriah, its most important and sacred hill, as the abode of the Lord and as the gathering place for all the House of Israel. Legend has it that the Holy Temple was built on the site of a threshing-floor on Mount Moriah that King David purchased from Ornan the Jebusite. Payment was collected from all twelve tribes so that all of Israel would have a share in Jerusalem and the Temple. Even though the borders of two tribes (Judah and Benjamin) passed through the Jerusalem area, the capital itself belonged to no tribe and was in effect a federal capital. (See Zeev Vinai, *Legends of Jerusalem,* Philadelphia: The Jewish Publication Society of America, 1973, pp. 64-75, 133).

18. For a contrary opinion, see Kutcher's impassioned plea for the architectural preservation of Jerusalem and an indictment of Western planning technology. Arthur Kutcher, *The New Jerusalem Planning and Politics,* London: Thames and Hudson Ltd., 1973, 128 pp.

19. The survey boundaries of unified Jerusalem are detailed in *AzKarat Yerushalayim* Harchavat Techum HaIria), (Hebrew), 1967, Minister of Interior, Hayim Moshe Shapira, June 28, 1967, 3 pp.

20. For a succinct discussion of Jerusalem's urban explosion and planning needs, see Nathaniel Lichfield, "Jerusalem Planning: A Progress Report," in *Jerusalem,* edited by Oesterreicher and Sinai, *op. cit.,* pp. 175-186.

21. Description and analysis of building styles and street patterns in the Old City and outside the wall is found in David H.K. Amiran, "The Development of Jerusalem, 1860-1970," and in I. Kimchi's "Aspects of the Human Ecology of Jerusalem." These articles appear in *Urban Geography of Jerusalem – A Companion Volume to the Atlas of Jerusalem,* Jerusalem: Massada Press, 1973, pp. 30-52 and 109-122.

22. Colonel Sir Charles W. Wilson, *Jerusalem, The Holy City* (Reprinted from the book originally published in 1880, under the title *Picturesque Palestine, Sinai and Egypt),* Jerusalem: Ariel Publishing Co., (no date), 120 pp.

23. The first Governor of Jerusalem, Ronald Storrs, enacted this decree through the McClean Plan. See S. Shapiro, "Planning Jerusalem: The First Generation, 1917-1968," in *Urban Geography of Jerusalem, op. cit.,* pp. 139-153. Historic concern with Jerusalem's building landscape is discussed by Davies *(The Gospel and the Land, op. cit.,* pp. 135-137), who cites *Numbers 19:14* "neither beams nor balconies nor sockets may project there over the public thoroughfares lest, by overshadowing, they give passage to corpse uncleanliness."

24. S. Shapiro, "Planning Jerusalem: The First Generation, 1917-1968," in *Urban Geography of Jerusalem, op. cit.,* pp. 141-147.

25. Dov Joseph, *The Faithful City, op. cit.,* p. 5.

26. Uzi Benziman, *Yerushalayim – Ir L'Lo Homa,* (Hebrew), Tel Aviv: Schocken Publishing House, Ltd., 1973, p. 253.

27. For a discussion and analysis of the process that attended the entire expropriation proceedings, see Benziman, *ibid.,* pp. 250-265.

28. Israel Kimchi, Benjamin Heyman, Claud Gabriel, *Yerushalayim, 1967-1975, Sekira Hevratit KalKalit,* (Hebrew), *(Socio-Economic Survey),* Hebrew University Institute for Urban and Regional Studies, Jerusalem Studies Center, April, 1976, p. 33.

29. Kimchi et. al., *ibid.,* note that official figures for those who register in the labor exchange dropped from a high of 8,300 in 1971 to 6,600 in 1975, but that the estimates of the true size of this work force are over 10,000 (p. 37).

30. Kimchi et. al., *ibid.,* p. 38.

From Peripheral to Focal: From Satellite to Competing Core

This chapter deals with two phenomena — the transformation of Jerusalem's location from that of peripheral to focal within Israel, and between Israel and the Arab West Bank; and the emergence of Jerusalem as a political core, potentially competitive with the Tel Aviv core area. These phenomena are not independent — they are causally related. The focal location that has triggered major growth and development, has also provided Jerusalem with a unique set of local political energies that can make an impact upon the politics and ideology of Israel as a whole.

WEST JERUSALEM — A PERIPHERAL ISRAELI CAPITAL

The shift in relative location of Jerusalem from peripheral to focal in Israel, has stimulated the city's growth in unprecedented fashion. With this shift, Jerusalem is rapidly becoming a competing political core to the Tel Aviv core within the Jewish state. It is also becoming focal, once again, to much of the Arab West Bank.

65

When Jerusalem became the capital of the new Jewish state in 1950, it was on the physical periphery. Largely surrounded by hostile Arab forces and short of buildable land, it was in danger of being pinched off from the coastal plain to which it was so tenuously tied. In spite of these negative conditions, from the very outset Israeli governmental policy was to develop Jerusalem as an administrative, educational and industrial center. The city was to be linked to the lowlands by a chain of settlements that would be established in what up to then was a narrow, nearly empty corridor, only ten to fifteen kilometers wide and with only three Jewish and two Arab villages. Ben Gurion summed up the task ahead at a meeting of the Provisional State Council on June 24, 1948, between the first and second truce periods of the War of Independence. "King David chose one of the most difficult places in the country for his capital. Those who returned to Zion in recent generations did not pay heed to a physical link to Jerusalem. By some miracle, a Jewish majority was maintained in the city, and recently it has grown larger. But it is not enough to have a Jewish majority inside the city; there must also be a Jewish agricultural hinterland and a road to Jerusalem lined with Jewish settlements. So far we are in control of a very narrow corridor. It must be enlarged in the north and in the south, and strengthened by the establishment of agricultural military settlements."[1]

In 1948, the picture was grim. Jerusalem's population at the end of the war had dropped to 70,000 from its 1947 level of 100,000. A number of factors were responsible for this decline. At the start of the siege many aged and infirm had vacated the city. Then during lulls in the fighting and at the end of the war, businessmen left because they could not make ends meet; many had not reopened the enterprises which had been closed during the siege. About half of all businesses were closed down for a six month period. The young went off to the armed forces, and half of the skilled workers left the city or their jobs. Moreover, with the emergence of a large governmental bureaucracy in Tel Aviv, many civil servants moved there. To stem the outward flow during the truce period, no one was allowed to leave without a special permit.[2] The net loss of population from the city was checked when Jewish immigrants were directed to settle in the capital. In 1950 alone, 30,000 immigrants came, many from Arabic lands of the Middle East and North Africa, and intensified a trend that would make Jerusalem a more heavily Oriental-North African Jewish city than either Tel Aviv or Haifa.

Revival of the City

Revival of the city encountered serious obstacles. The Jerusalem Economic Corporation was established to counteract chronic investment capital shortages. Its role was to establish industrial estates, which, in the early developmental stages, concentrated on the manufacture of shoes, textiles and pharmaceuticals, and on the expansion of printing and publishing. Jerusalem's economic stagnation could not be attributed solely to the war. In the 1920s and 1930s, the basically consumeristic nature of the city's economy and the absence of a vibrant manufacturing base had created serious problems. These had only been temporarily papered-over by the general prosperity brought to the city by military industry and tourist servicemen during World War II.[3] Other obstacles included the refusal of many foreign states to relocate their embassies in Jerusalem after it had been formally designated as the capital of Israel on January 30, 1950, and security problems along the Jordanian border that ringed the city.

Nevertheless, Jewish Jerusalem did grow during this 1948-67 period. Its population increased from the 1947 base of 100,000 to 195,000 at the outbreak of the Six Day War. Moreover, nearly fifty settlements with 30,000 people were established in the Corridor, which was administratively divided into two districts, one centering around Bet Shemesh at the western end and the other around Mevasseret Zion at the eastern edge of the Corridor. The Corridor's development began even before the fighting was completely finished. During the truce periods, stone houses were built as strongholds on key hills, the nuclei for villages later established.[4] The growth, however, was absolute and not relative to growth elsewhere in Israel.

Before 1948, Jerusalem had served as a commercial and business center for Upland Palestine (from Beersheba to Schechem), and, for certain administrative and educational services, for all of Palestine and also for Amman. The formal boundaries of the Jerusalem Planning District, as defined by the Palestine Mandate included the Jericho, Ramallah and Hebron subdistricts. To the north and south the lines extended within 20 kilometers of Nablus and Beersheba. Most of the west short of the Dead Sea was included in the east, and the western boundaries extended almost to the coastal plain (just to the east of Faluja, Qastina, Latrun and Lydda). Over the next two decades the city declined in national and regional significance. Jerusalem's commerce and services extended only the small and underpopulated Corridor starting at Bet Shemesh (see Figure 5).[5] Moreover, it had become an eccentric point in the pattern of distribution of Israel's population, and the internal development of West Jerusalem had been distorted by the armistice lines.

With only one possible direction of growth, westward, the built-up area could not spread out uniformly, but had to adapt to the hill-vale topography. Neighborhoods were built on hill-tops and ridges, separated from one another by valleys. This was cause for a highly elongated, interrupted settlement pattern that magnified distances from the center of the city and affected the cost and quality of urban services.[6] The distance of the Hadassah Medical Center at Ein Kerem, on the western edge of the city, eight kilometers from the population center, is an example of the problem of stretched lines of service communication. The Ein Kerem location problem has been exacerbated by the fact that post-1967 population growth has occurred in the northeast and southeast sections of the united city, putting a stop to the westward march of the center of gravity of population.

Indicative of Jewish Jerusalem's relative lag during this nineteen year period was its decline both in proportion of population to total national population, and in the share that Jerusalem received of gross national investment. Jerusalem's 1946 Jewish population of about 100,000 represented nearly 17% of the total Jewish population of Palestine while the unified city's population of 164,000 was 8.8% of the total population of the Mandated territory. With independence, West Jerusalem's share of the national Israeli population dropped steadily from 10% in 1948, leveling off at 7.4% before the outbreak of the Six Day War.

Table 2
Pre-Unification
Selected Years, Jerusalem's Share of Total Israeli Population

Year	Population of West Jerusalem	Population of Israel	West Jerusalem's % of National Population
1948	84,000	835,000	10.0
1949	104,000	1,174,000	8.9
1952	139,000	1,630,000	8.7
1961	165,000	2,234,000	7.4
1966	195,000	2,629,000	7.4

Related to a shrinking share of national population during the period of the city's division was the even smaller proportion of national investment received by West Jerusalem. It is estimated that in the 1950s, Jerusalem received three-to-four percent of the gross Israeli annual national investment. This increased to five-to-six percent in the first half of the 1960s (a peak of 6.1% in 1966),[7] but was still under national per capita investment norms. It should be added that direct governmental development investments were much higher proportionally, representing about 30% of total governmental investments during the first half of the 1960s. However, governmental impact was not enough to affect the gross investment picture materially. Both gross national and direct governmental capital investments in Jerusalem increased dramatically after 1967.

EAST JERUSALEM — STAGNATION UNDER THE JORDANIANS

In contrast to the modest growth of West Jerusalem, East Jerusalem under the control of Jordan experienced both economic and population decline. Like their Jewish counterparts, many Arabs had fled the city in 1948-49, but fewer returned. Moreover, negative migration balance over the next two decades countered natural increase from high birth rates. The continued Arab outflow from Jerusalem was attracted by jobs in the Arab world and elsewhere. While not large enough to compensate for the emigrants, there was a substantial inflow from other parts of the West Bank, especially Hebron. Indeed the Muslim Hebronites who were lower income shopkeepers, artisans and workers, became a major element within the walls of the Old City. They replaced higher income Christians and Muslims who either moved their businesses outside the walls, or emigrated from the country.

Various censuses of the population of Jordanian Jerusalem show a decline from 78,000 in 1946, to 52,000 in 1952. The population increased to 60,000 in 1961, and was measured at 66,000 in 1967. In fact, however, the 1967 figure that was comparable to the 1961 statistic was only 44,000. The remainder was the population from surrounding villages that were incorporated into the city when Israeli authorities expanded the corporate limits after reunification.[8]

Contributing to the stagnation of Jerusalem was the Jordanian government's policy of emphasizing the economic and administrative growth of Amman. This occurred despite King 'Abdallah's great attachment to Jerusalem, the government's proclamation of Jerusalem as the alternate capital of the Hashemite Kingdom (August 6, 1953), and Hussein's declaration of his intention to live in Jerusalem part of the time. Hussein announced this intention in 1954, but did not lay the cornerstone for his palace until a decade later.[9] In fact, except for substantial investments in tourism, almost no economic attention was paid by the Jordanians to Jerusalem. Tourism did make impressive strides during this period. The more than half million visitors who came to Jerusalem generated half of all Jordan's annual tourist revenues, and supported a thriving hotel, guide, transportation and specialized shopping industry. The remarkable growth of Amman (from 22,000 in 1948, to a quarter of a million in 1961, to 330,000 in 1967, to an estimated 675,000 in 1975) attracted many of Jerusalem's Muslim businessmen and former Mandatory civil servants. Christian Arabs were less prone to seek out the relatively inhospitable atmosphere of Muslim Amman, and, with economic stagnation in Jerusalem, left to go abroad in large numbers. Thus, the Christian Arab population of the city dropped from 31,000 in 1946, to 10,795 in the 1967 census, or from about 45% of the non-Jewish population to 17%.

East Jerusalem's stagnation may also in part be attributed to competition from other West Bank towns. While Arab Jerusalem continued to supply some public services to the rest of the West Bank, and increased its tourist vitality, it lost ground both to Nablus and Hebron as an industrial and commercial center. The population of Nablus in 1952 was 42,000. It grew to 46,000 in 1961, and was 50,000 in 1975. Hebron, with 36,000 in 1952, had grown to 45,000 in 1975. Each of the cities experienced even more rapid growth in surrounding urbanized villages and towns. Powerful local political and merchant forces had made Nablus a pulsating center for nationalist and economic activities, in contradistinction to Jerusalem. Moreover, even the local tributary area of East Jerusalem was diminished, at least temporarily, when the demarcation line cut the road to Bethlehem. Until an alternate two-lane highway was built in 1952-53 via Silwan and

Sur Bahir, there were no direct links to Bethlehem and Hebron. This road cut through the eastern and southern edges of the Government House Demilitarized Zone, and was overlooked from the kibbutz of Ramat Rahel.

The 1948-67 period can be summed up this way: despite persistent and major efforts by the Israeli government to develop West Jerusalem as a frontier capital, the Israeli city's relative growth did not keep pace with that of Israel as a whole. Jerusalem was no longer the upland junction that it had been from the time that King David made it his capital, to the moment of the departure of the British Mandatory Authority on May 14, 1948. It had become an outlier — a "dead end" at the eastern tip of a corridor cul de sac. But the effort to maintain and develop a powerful Jewish presence in Jerusalem persisted throughout this period despite the obstacles. The same does not apply to the Arab commitment to East Jerusalem. Deprived by the Hashemite government of the political and economic tools necessary to strengthen their presence, Palestinian Arabs lacked the opportunity to build up their base in Jerusalem. By 1967, West Jerusalem was a large Jewish city primed for the developments that changing military and political conditions would permit. From an Israeli perspective, the fruits of the unity of the Holy City belonged to those who had not abandoned it in its period of low ebb.

REUNIFICATION — CATALYST FOR DEVELOPMENT

The temporary lowering of Jerusalem's locational status changed abruptly in 1967. Reunification of the city as a result of the Six Day War, with full access both to the coastal plain and to the West Bank, restored Jerusalem's focal location. What followed reunification was an unprecedented burst of economic activity and population growth. Jerusalem's share of the Israeli national population has nearly returned to the 1948 10% level. Moreover, unified Jerusalem's share of the combined population of Israel and the West Bank is about 8.2%, close to the same proportion that it was at the end of the Palestine Mandate. This growth has had two effects: (1) it has made Jerusalem an overwhelmingly Jewish city, more so than at any other point in modern times; (2) it has caused the old Walled City to become dwarfed in population and area, relative to the rest of Jerusalem. The geopolitical impact of Jerusalem's emergence as a largely Jewish city, with a population not restricted to Western Jerusalem but distributed in East Jerusalem and the Old City, is a new reality. This reality has to be taken into account in addressing Arab demands for repartition of the city or in considering Christian proposals for internationalization.

Population Growth

Reunification has served as a catalytic force for Israeli development of the city. Jewish population has grown as a result of internal immigration, the magnet-like appeal of Jerusalem to immigrants from abroad, and the conscious governmental policy of directing settlement by increasing the housing stock. Economic development has been spurred by a combination of tourism, governmental and institutional growth, building and manufacturing.

While West Jerusalem prior to 1967 had been steadily decreasing in its share of the total national population (See Table 3), since unification the city has been growing at a rate of 3.7% per annum. Its 1975 population of 356,000 represented 10.2% of Israel's 1975 populace. It should be noted that Jerusalem's 1975 Jewish population of 259,000, 7.4% of the nation's total, is a figure that is more directly comparable with pre-1967 figures presented in Table 2.

Between 1967 and 1974, 22,500 immigrants from abroad settled in Jerusalem. Net internal migration has not been nearly so high, numbering 6,700 during this same period. Nevertheless, the latter figure is significant because net outward migration characterized Jerusalem in several years of the previous decade, including 1965 and 1966, when the net loss was 1,700. Jerusalem's absorption of Jewish immigrants is very much related to its attractiveness to religious and intellectual circles. Reinforcing this natural attractiveness has been governmental policy in providing housing and jobs. During the 1970s, Jerusalem has absorbed an annual average of 8% of all Jewish immigrants to the country in contrast with 4.5% per annum for the 1960s. Official goals for the coming years are to have Jerusalem absorb 10% of all Jewish immigrants, a figure that was met in 1974.

Table 3
Post-Unification
Jerusalem's Share of Total Israeli Population

Year	Population of Jerusalem			Population of Israel	Jerusalem's % of National Population	
	Total	Jewish	Non-Jewish		Total Jerusalem Population	Jewish Jerusalem Population
1967	266,000	198,000	69,000	2,715,000	9.8	7.3
1968	275,000	203,000	72,000	2,807,000	9.8	7.2
1969	283,000	209,000	74,000	2,884,000	9.8	7.2
1970	292,000	216,000	76,000	2,974,000	9.8	7.3
1971	301,000	222,000	79,000	3,069,000	9.8	7.2
1972	320,000	235,000	85,000	3,173,000	10.1	7.4
1973	331,000	243,000	88,000	3,277,000	10.1	7.4
1974	344,000	251,000	93,000	3,369,000	10.2	7.4
1975	356,000	259,000	97,000	3,490,000	10.2	7.4

Employment and Investment

The significance to Jerusalem of growth through migration from abroad is tied to the absolute size of this migration. Reunification of Jerusalem was followed shortly by the wave of Jewish migration from the U.S.S.R. Nearly 90,000 immigrants came in the three years, from 1971 to 1973. With the sudden drop of this immigration in 1974 to 17,000, and then to 8,500 in 1975, and in the absence of increases from other parts of the world, Jerusalem's Jewish growth rate will have to depend much more on trends in internal migration. A leveling off in growth of the Hebrew University and of certain public non-governmental institutions has decreased the population support base. Proposed relocation to Jerusalem of the Histadrut could mean a boost in internal migration. This is a move that has long been contemplated and now seems to be in the offing. But this move aside, only a major shift in governmental policy that would relocate the defense ministry from Tel Aviv to Jerusalem, is likely to stimulate a new substantial flow of internal Jewish migrants. Opposition to such a move comes both from a security standpoint and because of forces of inertia including objections to relocation by employees.

Thus, a slow-down in growth of Jerusalem's Jewish population may well take place during the second decade of reunification. Only a drastic change in employment patterns or an unexpected revival of immigration from abroad could alter the situation. In Jerusalem, Jews are occupying increasingly lower proportions of the job market in industry, personal services and building. In 1968, 35% of Jewish employees were engaged in the above sectors, while in 1975, the figure had declined to 24%. The comparable employment figures for Jerusalem's Arab population in these sectors were 43% in 1968, and 38% in 1975.[10] Drift of the Jewish population away from basic jobs in industry, building and personal services is not unique to Jerusalem; it is a national phenomenon. Arab labor from the West Bank as well as Israel has moved dramatically into these sectors of the economy, to the point where many Jews are voicing their anxiety about the loss of Zionist ideals of self-labor and self-realization. A change in Jewish employment trends depends upon two factors: 1) basic shift in individual goals, ideals and perceptions of work values, and 2) sudden closing off of employment opportunities and social security benefits to Arabs.[11] In either case, the issues are nationwide ones, not ones that can be solved through the specific addressing of Jerusalem's problems. In the face of needs to find long-term accommodation with Israel's Arab citizens, perhaps they are insoluble.

Jewish population growth of the past decade has depended very much upon the inflow of national investment. It was previously noted that in the few years prior to reunification, Jerusalem was receiving 5% to 6% of gross national investment and about 30% of total direct governmental investments. The gross national investment increased to 8.9% in 1967, went as high as 16.5% in 1971, and has averaged 12% for the past few years, or more than double its first-half of the 1960s rate. Direct governmental development investments have also increased dramatically, averaging 42% in the past few years, with one annual peak of 48%.[12] Construction (for residences and public institutions), tourism (hotels and services), industry, transportation, and telecommunications have received the investment in that order, half of all investments being in residential and public institutional building, and over one-fifth in hotels.

ARAB PRESENCE IN JERUSALEM

In dealing with a two-level system, the Israeli and the Israeli-Palestinian Arab, the growth of Jewish Jerusalem must also be considered in the context of developments in the Arab sector. From 1948 to 1967, the patterns of growth of the two communities were contradictory. The first sharp reduction in Jerusalem's Arab population came during and after the War of Independence. While West Jerusalem was growing in numbers and in economic vitality, the Arab section declined. The assymetry between Jewish and Arab growth patterns intensified immediately after the Six Day War when there occurred another major drop in the Arab population. This was statistically papered-over to some degree by the absorption of new Arab areas within the municipality that had previously not been part of Jordanian East Jerusalem.

Population Trends

The 1967 Israeli census of East Jerusalem showed a severe loss of population within the Jordanian city boundaries. While the

1961 Jordanian census enumerated 60,000 persons, the Israeli census found only 44,000 (a drop of 27%). The Old City was especially hard-hit dropping from 37,000 to 24,000, (or by 36%). There was some compensation for this loss from the suburbs annexed in 1967, which increased in population to 21,000 from an estimated 15,000 in 1961. All in all, the unified Jerusalem in its new boundaries had a population of 66,000 Arabs compared to the estimated 75,000 for the same area in 1961. The decrease in population could not be attributed solely to flight in the wake of the Six Day War, when it is estimated that 18% of the Arab population left the city. Population erosion had proceeded through much of the 1948-67 period, the general net outflow ranging anywhere from 1-to-5% per annum.[13]

When the two sectors were finally reunited in 1967, the Arab population had dropped to 25.8% of the city's total. During the previous half century, Arabs had constituted a larger proportional entity, although since the 1860s, Jews had been the single largest group in Jerusalem. From 1967 to 1970, the Arabs continued to represent one-quarter of the population total. There was reason to assume that the opposing trends of Jewish and Arab growth patterns would continue — that growth of the former would mean decline of the latter. However, beginning in 1968, Arabs ceased to leave Jerusalem. In addition, reunification of families and continued in-migration from the West Bank, especially the Hebron area, began to make their impact. This, coupled with a high rate of natural increase (30 per thousand from 1967-72, and 35 per thousand since then, compared to 20 per thousand for Jerusalem's Jews) has begun to increase the proportionate share of the city's Arab population (See Table 4).

With Arab population increasing at a rate of 4.5% per annum since reunification, and the Jewish population at 3.5%, the Arab presence now has a more solid base. Much of the Arab growth can be explained in terms of higher birth rates in the suburban agricultural villages that were absorbed within Jerusalem's boundaries. As these families become increasingly urbanized, their fertility rates may be expected to drop. In 1961, the then largely urbanized Arab East Jerusalem had a natural increase of only 2.8%. Natural birth rate aside, speculation about the future of the Arab presence in Jerusalem must take into account economic conditions, housing, educational opportunities, and the political-military situation. While these topics will be considered later, it should be noted that efforts to date to serve the needs of Jerusalem's Arab population have reflected more of a municipal commitment than a national Israeli commitment. From the standpoint of an Israeli strategy for peace that is based on accommodation initiatives, Israeli national investment for Jerusalem's Arabs in housing and the rest of the urban infrastructure would be highly desirable. Indeed such an investment would yield as many political dividends as would certain expensive military emplacements in the Sinai that are put up as much for purposes of political bargaining as they are for security.

Table 4[14]

Arab and Jewish Share of Jerusalem's Population

	Arab Population (%)	*Jewish Population (%)*
1922	45.6	54.4
1931	42.2	57.8
1946	39.6	60.4
1952	25.0	75.0
1961	27.6	72.4
1967	25.8	74.2
1968	26.1	73.9
1969	26.2	73.8
1970	26.1	73.9
1971	26.3	73.7
1972	26.6	73.4
1973	26.6	73.4
1974	27.1	72.9
1975	27.2	72.8

The Old City

The Old City, meanwhile, has become more and more of a "treasure house" enclave. Its population relative to the total population of Jerusalem has declined from 20% at the end of 1946, to 16% in 1961, to 9% in 1967, to less than 6% today. Its land area, never large relative to the modern city that developed outside its walls in the nineteenth century, is about a square kilometer. In 1922, Old Jerusalem was about 5% of the municipal area. By 1948, this figure had decreased to 2.5%. Today, the

Walled City occupies only 1% of the post-1967 new municipal area of 104 square kilometers. The decline of the Old City as living space, places greater emphasis on its role as a religious and commercial center. By rebuilding some of its residential sections, efforts are underway to prevent the Walled City from becoming a "museum." As long as it remains a residential center, it is not practical to conceive of a political fate for Old Jerusalem that is administratively separate from the city which surrounds it. On the other hand, functional international status for the Holy Places may be even more feasible, as the pressure of other activities, economic and residential, are decreased.

METROPOLIS AND CITY-REGION

To speak of Jerusalem's growth potential is to speak not only of the city, but also of its metropolitan area and even of the city-region. Jerusalem has reached out to both with its increasing significance as a daily commutation labor shed for the West Bank towns and villages of its periphery, and with the development of suburban housing in Jewish villages to the west of the city, and Arab villages in the north, east and south.

The Metropolitan Area

Jerusalem municipal planners include the southern half of the Ramallah district from Bir Zeit to Saffa to Beit Nuba and including Ramallah-Bira as being within the northern metropolitan reaches of the city. The southern reaches contain the north-western part of the Bethlehem district (from Bethlehem-Beit Jalah-Beit Sahur to the Etzion bloc settlements, Tekoa, Herodion, and Nabi Musa). The farthest metropolitan reach from Jerusalem to the north and to the south is 12 kilometers; to the west it is 30 and to the east, 17 kilometers (see Figure 8).[15] The city-region as defined by Israel's Ministry of Interior is the Jerusalem District, i.e., the Corridor and the city.

Metropolitan Jerusalem is much more balanced in population composition than is the city or the Jerusalem Planning District. Indeed, because the majority of the towns and villages in the metropolis outside of Jerusalem is Arab (85% in 1974, with only 15% being Jewish), the total metropolitan population including

Jerusalem is nearly fifty-fifty in its mix. In 1967, the population of 427,000 was 47% Arab. This proportion slowly increased so that by 1975, of 554,000 people, 48.6% were Arab. During this nine year period, the metropolitan area excluding the municipality had an increase in Arab population from 133,000 to 179,000, while the Jewish population rose from 28,000 to 31,000. The total population of the metropolitan area rose in the same nine year period from 161,000 to 209,000.[16]

Increase in the metropolitan Arab population is essentially a function of high natural birth rates among the villagers. To date, this rapid growth has not challenged the city's dominance within the metropolitan area because of Jerusalem's combination of high natural increases and immigration. Thus, the metropolitan population of 161,000 was 38% of the total population of 427,000 in 1967, and in 1974, it remained at 38% (209,000 out of 554,000). In the future, the city's population may be reduced proportionally, if Jewish immigration decreases, and as the urbanizing Arab population of East Jerusalem reduces its family size.

Trends towards balancing the Arab-Jewish population within the metropolitan area, as well as reducing the dominance of Jerusalem as a central city, may have significant geopolitical implications. If certain metropolitan, functional political structures can be developed on a "one person-one vote" basis, Arabs can begin to perceive themselves on a par with Jews. Both in psychological as well as political terms, Arabs may then be more willing to help establish the second order of the system — i.e., the special-type, functional administrative geopolitical system that links both Israel and the Arab West Bank.

The City-Region

But even Metropolitan Jerusalem is too limited a concept to embrace Jerusalem's outreach potential — the potential of the Jerusalem city-region. During the first quarter of a century of Israeli independence, Jerusalem, the provincial outpost, was linked to the coastal plain by a string of rural settlements. Now, a role may be forecast for Jerusalem as a focus for urbanization, the impact of which will be felt on upland and coastal areas thirty to forty kilometers distant. Beyond Jerusalem's metropolitan Arab suburbs and satellite cities, Jerusalem's economic and social reach is to the eastern Judean Desert, the northern end of the Dead Sea, Hebron and much of the northern part of the Ramallah

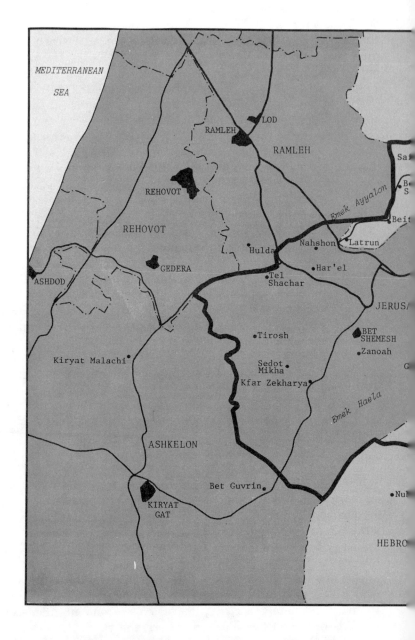

Fig. 8. Metropolitan Jerusalem

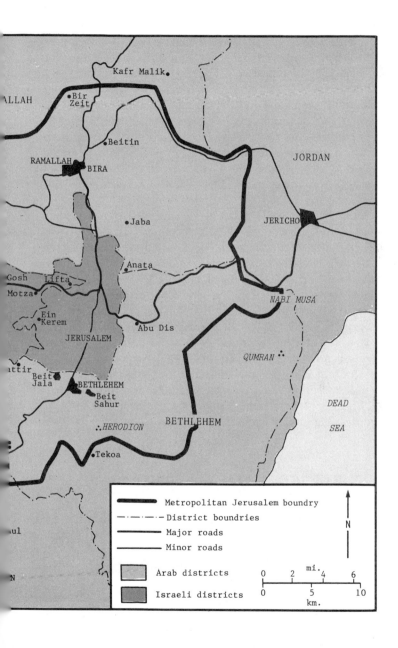

Kafr Malik

Bir Zeit

ALLAH

Beitin

RAMALLAH BIRA

JORDAN

Jaba

JERICHO

Gosh Lifta
Motza

Anata

NABI MUSA

Ein
Kerem

Abu Dis

JERUSALEM

QUMRAN

attir Beit
Jala

Beit
Sahur

BETHLEHEM

BETHLEHEM

HERODION

DEAD

SEA

Tekoa

sul

Metropolitan Jerusalem boundry

District boundries

Major roads

Minor roads

N

Arab districts

Israeli districts

mi.
0   2   4   6

0   5   10
km.

district (see Figure 9). The Jewish sector of the city-region has an even broader extent. Growth pressures both westward from Jerusalem and eastward from the Israeli Center (i.e., the area centering around Tel Aviv that extends from Netania to Rehovot to Lod-Ramleh) may be expected to fill the Shefelah (Piedmont) and selected portions of the Upland Corridor.

The Shefelah sector around Bet Shemesh and Latrun are likely to attract major development, especially as national pressures mount to protect the overcrowded coastal plain from additional residential, industrial and transportation uses. Final stretches of the modern highway from the Center to the capital are under construction, and some of the Corridor's rural settlements are already beginning to convert to urban functions. By the end of Israel's next quarter of a century, a central upland region to include the Shefelah (Latrun-Emek Ayyalon and Bet Shemesh-Nahal Soreq), the mountain passageway, and Metropolitan Jerusalem is likely to embrace a population of well over one million and could be a continuous part of Israel's Central Region. The Jerusalem District Plan calls for a 1992 population of 565,000 for the city and 80,000 for the Corridor.[17] This does not take into account growth potential in the Arab metropolitan areas north and south of the city (current population 175,000), let alone what development may occur in Latrun-Emek Ayyalon. Clearly, a city-region embracing Jerusalem urbanites, suburban and satellite townspeople, and agricultural villagers, and having approximately equally Jewish and Arab populations could be a very effective link between Israel and Arab Palestine.

DECLINE OF JERUSALEM AS A POLITICAL CENTER

The political consequences of this new focal location for Jerusalem feed back to the politics and ideology of the Israeli state. As long as it was peripheral, even as a capital, Jerusalem was less an independent generator and more a recipient of Israeli political ideals. Most national capitals are part of a state's political core area, but frontier Jerusalem was not during the 1948-69 period. Because of the conditions under which Zionist settlement developed during the Mandatory period, Jerusalem was not even the political core for Jewish Palestine then.

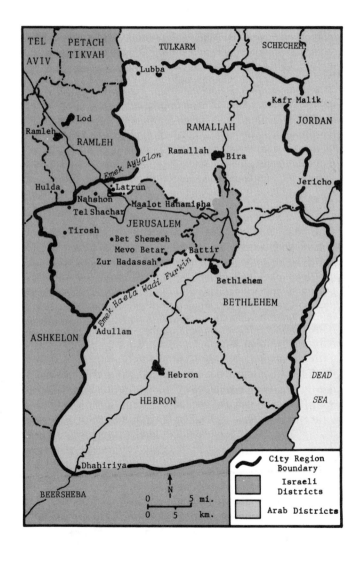

Fig. 9. The Jerusalem City-Region

The Zionist return found Jerusalem a religious rather than a political center. Jebusite stronghold, City of David, Capital of the First and Second Kingdoms of Judea, Aelia Capitolina during the Roman-Byzantine period, Capital of the Crusader Domains, at times referred to in their entirety as the "Latin Kingdom of Jerusalem" — Jerusalem had long ago experienced glory as a political power base, and then for hundreds of years lost all semblance of political significance.

Never a great center of Mameluke government (it was regarded as an honorable place of banishment for emirs), Jerusalem did not share the capital status of Gaza, Safed, or Ramleh, but was a regional seat (amal) in Mamlakat Damascus. During the Ottoman rule, Jerusalem (Al-Kuds) served as district capital for Sanjak Al-Kuds, one of the southern sanjaks of the Vilayet of Damascus. Its hinterland was largely limited to the Judean Upland, with Hebron (Al-Khalil) as the only other important town. To the north, east and west lay the more important sanjaks of Nablus and Gaza. The Negev (Beersheba) was outside the Ottoman administrative framework. Towards the mid-nineteenth century, the Jerusalem sanjak was shifted to the Sidon Vilayet, as the Palestinian coast grew in power and importance. While during much of the Ottoman era, some towns in Palestine (Acre, Safed, Jaffa) experienced periods of political or commercial glory as centers for autonomous regions, this was not the case for Jerusalem.[18] Isolated, exposed to Bedouin attack from the Judean desert on the east and along the roads to its south and the west, Jerusalem remained a backwater area.

It is important to note that the Ottomans did not neglect Jerusalem's defenses, despite its political insignificance. During the eighteenth century, when the Turkish army in Palestine experienced declining fortunes owing to general neglect and inflexibility by the Sublime Porte, Jerusalem continued to be manned by a considerable garrison, in comparison with the other Palestinian towns.[19] Religious and historical factors were behind this military decision by the declining central authority.

Modern Zionist settlement at the end of the Ottoman reign, therefore, found Jerusalem with almost no political authority. For matters of crucial importance in dealing with Turkish authorities, it was necessary to journey to Damascus. And for contacts with the Western world, Jaffa's consulates and post offices were the important outlets.

Because it was the center of the "Old Yishuv" (pre-Zionist settlement) and the main Jewish town of Palestine (with over half the total Jewish population), Jerusalem was not completely devoid of some Jewish political activity during this last stage of the Ottoman period. The infant labor parties opened their offices and their press in Jerusalem. In 1914, before their exile from Palestine, an attempt was made by labor leaders Ben Zvi, R. Yanait and Ben Gurion to establish a militia in Jerusalem. Hebrew publishing activities increased in Jerusalem, and Jewish representatives met Turkish military and civilian authorities there, when not being summoned to Damascus.

Coastal Plain Beginnings

Even during the Turkish occupation, Jewish colonizing efforts were taking up headquarters locations on the coast, not in Jerusalem. In 1908, Arthur Ruppin emigrated to Palestine as representative of the Zionist Organization. He set up the Palestine Office on Bustrus Street, the main street of Jaffa. The office Ruppin directed served as the Palestinian headquarters of the Zionist Organization and its various institutions, such as the Jewish National Fund, the Palestine Land Development Corporation and the Palestine Real Estate Company. Ruppin cited a number of reasons for choosing Jaffa: 1) it was already head office for the Anglo-Palestine Company (founded in 1903 as the first Jewish bank in Palestine), the Odessa Committee of the Hovevi Zion (Lovers of Zion), and the Geulah land development corporation; 2) it was centrally located among the largest Jewish agricultural settlements; and most important 3) it contained the greater part of the "New Yishuv." Jaffa's Jews numbered 8,000 out of the total of about 20,000 Jewish colonists living in Palestine after thirty years of pioneering efforts. Ruppin observes that "Haifa had a much smaller number of recent settlers, and in Jerusalem the newcomers went unnoticed among the large majority of the Old Yishuv."[20] Jerusalem was not only off-center; it was difficult to get to. It was four to six hours by train (over 87 kilometers of tracks), and ten to fourteen hours by horse and carriage over a rutted road that had been built only in 1869. Moreover, Jerusalem was *politically* alien to the new Jewish settlers for it contained a majority of the 50,000 Jews of the Old Yishuv of Palestine. A large proportion of them lived on Halukah (charity) funds from abroad, and were impoverished and hostile on religious and traditional grounds to the Zionist return. Jerusalem was not a favorable political center for the New Yishuv.

The Zionist Presence in Jerusalem under the Mandate

To a certain extent, the situation changed with the Balfour Declaration of November 2, 1917, and the conquest of Jerusalem by General Allenby's forces the following month. Jerusalem became the British Headquarters and capital. The San Remo Conference of April, 1920, entrusted the Mandate of the government of Palestine to Great Britain, with responsibility for putting the Declaration into effect of establishing in Palestine a national home for the Jewish people. Article 4 of the League of Nations Mandate called for "an appropriate Jewish agency as a public body for advising and cooperating with the Administration of Palestine in such economic, social and other matters as may affect the establishment of the Jewish national home . . . ."[21]

The Zionist Organization was recognized in the articles of the Mandate as the Jewish Agency. It was logical therefore that its efforts should shift from Jaffa to Jerusalem. A year before San Remo, the Zionist Commission had been appointed to direct all Zionist affairs in Palestine, replacing Ruppin's Palestine Office, and moving its activities to Jerusalem. Two years later the commission became the Zionist Executive. It acted also as the recognized Jewish Agency, until an expanded body, including non-Zionist representatives known as the Jewish Agency for Palestine, was created in 1929.

Moving to Jerusalem with the Zionist Commission as associated Zionist bodies were the Jewish National Fund (founded in 1901), and the Palestine Foundation Fund (1921). Housed in the same building compound as the Zionist organizations was the Vaad Leumi, the National Council created in 1920 as the Council of the Assembly (Assefat Nivcharim) representing the various parties of Jewish Palestine. Important educational, religious and social institutions were also established in Jerusalem, especially the Chief Rabbinate office in 1921, and the Hebrew University which was inaugurated in 1925.

Despite its function as headquarters for Zionist political organizations, Jerusalem did not become Jewish Palestine's political nerve center. The British Mandatory Capital was not a conducive setting for the development of political instruments which could take active command of the struggle to build a state and forge independence. The Mandatory Government was biased in favor of employing Arabs. Most of its medium and lower-level bureaucrats were Arab (the top level was English), and Jews were afforded few opportunities as training ground for developing a national bureaucracy. In addition to Jerusalem's being the focus of British opposition to statehood, it was the home of Hajj Amin al Huseini, Mufti in Jerusalem. Appointed to this post by the High Commissioner in 1921, and becoming chief of the Supreme Moslem Council the following year, he conducted a war against Zionism from the Holy City. Riot upon riot was inspired by the Mufti. Eventually Huseini was to turn against the British as well as the Jews, allying himself with Nazi Germany, and fleeing to Germany in World War II.

ORIGINS OF THE YISHUV'S MODERN POLITICAL CORE AREA

Lacking a secure base in Jerusalem, the most important Palestinian Jewish Organizations — the Histadrut (the General Federation of Workers in Eretz Israel), and the National High Command of the Hagana (the Jewish Defense Forces) — took up their operational bases in Tel Aviv. Here, with access to modern Jewish settlement on the coast and in the north, developed the political nerve center of the embryonic Jewish state (See Figure 10).

The concept of a political core area derives from a physicalistic view of the national state, a view which treats the state as an organism built around a single nucleus, or, in certain exceptional cases, multiple nuclei. The relationship between core and periphery varies: sometimes interaction is one-way, or exploitative, with the core feeding off the periphery by drawing upon its natural resources; at other times, the core may have to support all, or a portion of the periphery, so that there is net outflow of resources from the core; and still at other times, the relationship between core and periphery is two-way or interdependent. Whatever the case, it is assumed that the character of the core is a major element in nation-building and in shaping national policy.

The political core may be defined as a unique area whose residents influence national political values and mold national political structures and institutions. The set of man-land relations that

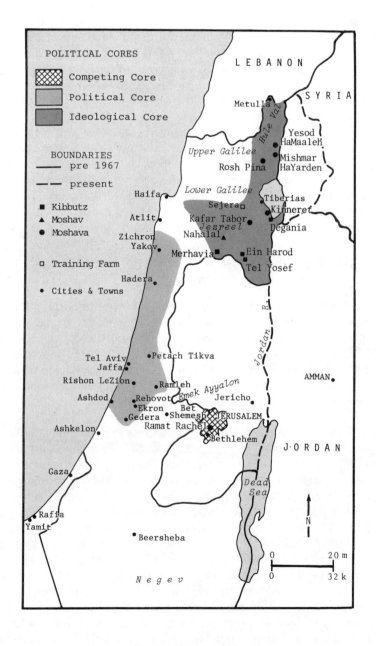

Fig. 10. Political Cores of Israel

exists in the political core shapes the tone, quality and substance of its ideological values which, in turn, then permeates the entire national territory. These values have to do with such overall issues as allocation of resources, attitudes towards external contacts and defense. Those who develop the national goals do not all have to live in the core, but they do have to identify with its environmental qualities and ethos.

The North

In the case of Israel, the nuclear (historic) core area and ideological base of the modern state emerged during the first third of the twentieth century. Locus initially was the North: the fringes of the Galilee, the Upper Jordan Valley, the Valley of Jezreel. For a variety of reasons early Socialist-Zionist immigration waves were attracted there and the region became the central stage for the agricultural pioneering movement. The Second Aliya (1904-1914) and the Third Aliya (1919-1923) were immigration waves dominated by those committed to the concept of conquest of the land. These "founding fathers" eventually created the labor parties and organizations that fashioned the national myths, staffed the bureaucracy and shaped the Zionist state.

Both myth and geopolitical reality directed the attention northward. There the pioneers first came in search of a landscape with some resemblance to the forested, humid eastern or grassy southern Russian rural milieu, rejecting both the noise and squalor of Arab Jaffa, and the paternalism that characterized their relations with farm owners in the coastal Jewish colonies. On moving to Sejera in 1908, the young immigrant David Ben Gurion said: "The constant work with the hoe (in a coastal plain colony) did not entirely satisfy me. There was the scent of workshops in this dull, unceasing thud of the hoe. I yearned for spacious fields, for waving corn, for the scent of herbage and the song of the ploughman; and so it was that I resolved to go to the Galilee. Here in Sejera I found that Homeland for which I longed so greatly . . . . There was opportunity to think and envision and dream."[22]

Three years later, Arthur Ruppin, the guiding organizational genius behind Zionist settlement and the major supporter of cooperative pioneering, was to say: "Now I dream of creating a Jewish centre by Lake Kinneret, of making Lake Kinneret 'Jewish'. Actually, this is not such a difficult problem, as the two larger towns, Tiberias and Safed are already Jewish. It would be enough to establish ten to twenty settlements on 100,000 to 200,000 dunams near Tiberias and provide the Jews of Tiberias and Safed with an assured income by introducing arts and crafts in order for them to gain the upper hand. I would like to live to see at least that much, even if I am resigned to not seeing the whole of Palestine as a Jewish land. That task will remain for our children and grandchildren!"[23] By 1907, at the start of Ruppin's activities, the Galilee already contained in excess of 15,000 Jews; Ruppin hoped to double that figure in his Zionist development planning.[24]

That geopolitical considerations also strongly influenced this pull to the North was illustrated by a statement by Ben Gurion in 1921. "It is necessary that the water sources, upon which the future of the land depends, should not be outside the borders of the future Jewish homeland. . . . For this reason we have always demanded that the Land of Israel include the southern banks of the Litani River, the headwaters of the Jordan, and the Hauran Region from the El Adja spring south of Damascus. All the rivers run from east to west or from north to south. This explains the importance of the Upper Galilee and the Hauran for the entire country. The most important rivers of the Land of Israel are the Jordan, the Litani and the Yarmuk. The Land needs this water. Moreover, the development of industry depends on water power for the generation of electricity."[25] Col. Richard Meinertzhagen, the English soldier and diplomat who was so passionately devoted to the Zionist cause, made this same argument in a letter to Lord Curzon in 1919.[26]

Chief among the values of the Jewish pioneers of the North were settlement, immigration, Jewish labor, self defense, self sufficiency, self labor and cooperation. Jewish agricultural workers who had come to the Lower Galilee to work in Jewish farm colonies undertook the first experiments in self-management. In 1907 and 1908, the ICA (Jewish Colonization Association) farm at Sejera was organized by placing management of the farm in the hands of a workers' committee. In the fall of 1909, the Palestine Office signed a contract with disgruntled workers at the colony of Kinneret, permitting them to farm the land of Um Juni cooperatively. A year later, the workers renamed the settlement Degania, and established it as the first fullblown collective — a kvutza.[27]

Bar Giora, the secret defense society and forerunner of Hashomer was conceived at a meeting in Jaffa (September 1907), and proceeded to set up its base of operations in the Galilee at Sejera.[28] In 1909, in the Jewish village of Mescha (Kfar Tabor), the decision was taken by Bar Giora leaders, the collective at Sejera and the leaders of the Russian Jewish self-defense movement who had just arrived in Palestine, to reorganize in the form of a broadened, more open self-defense force, Hashomer. Members of Hashomer, in turn, participated in the establishment of Degania. Finally, in 1911, a federation of agricultural workers of the Galilee was established — in the same year a Judean agricultural workers federation was organized in Petach Tikva. These became major bases for the later development of the Histadrut. From these locally tested values emerged broader concepts that were to shape the state: Jewish national self-sufficiency independent of indigenous Arab and Mandatory forces; ingathering of the exiles; a popular defense army; and a workers' commonwealth. A decade later, the North, in which were concentrated 28 of the country's 57 Jewish agricultural settlements, was to spawn the Gdud HaAvoda (the Legion of Labor), the Hagana and the Histadrut.[29]

Shift to the Center

The northern core did not emerge in isolation. Instead, it built upon and displaced an incipient coastal plain node which had been created by the Jewish colonization wave of the First Aliya (starting in 1881-82). Farm settlements on a private basis had been established by immigrant groups associated with the Hovevi Zion. Lacking in funds they would have gone under had they not been taken over by Baron Edmond de Rothschild, and given financial support and direct management. While a few of the colonies were in the Galilee (Rosh Pina, Metullah, Yessod Ha-Maaleh, Mishmar HaYarden), most were spread over the coastal plain (Petach Tikva, Rishon LeZion, Zichron Yakov, Gedera, Rehovot, Hadera, Ekron).[30] Jaffa's Jewish population served as the commercial focus for these private farm colonies, and after the turn of the century, as has been noted, housed the Palestine Office. When, in 1900, Baron Rothschild transferred control of his settlements in Palestine to the ICA, the new management put greater emphasis on finding ways of making the villages self-supporting. Non-Zionist ICA centered much of its activity (1901-

1907) in the Lower Galilee, creating the training farm at Sejera and helping to establish the base upon which the cooperative Zionist Organization-supported pioneering effort of 1908-1920 was built.

But if the coastal plain was eclipsed by the political dynamism of the North, it continued to grow as the population core area and the economic base of the new Yishuv during this period. Jewish economic institutional life became centralized in the coastal plain, first with the establishment of the Anglo-Palestine Bank and then, in 1908, with the establishment of the Palestine Office's Palestine Land Development Company. The P.L.D.C. assumed responsibility for making all land purchases on behalf of ICA, the Anglo-Palestine Company and the Geula Company. Thus, it was able to coordinate land acquisition by these agencies with those of the Jewish National Fund, a Zionist institution.

An important educational landmark was the Herzlia Gymnasium opened in Tel Aviv in 1909. From this only Jewish high school in the country, Herzlia's graduates would one day become a major element of the elite, taking a prominent role in Gdud HaAvoda, the Legion of Labor (established in Tiberias in 1920). This Legion contributed to the absorption of hundreds of immigrants. But far more than its enlisting 2,500 members during the nine years of its existence, it shaped the socialistic ideals of the Third Aliya to include industry as well as agriculture. From its ranks came many of the founders and leaders of the Hagana.[31] The Legion initially was organized in small groups which worked in industry as well as agriculture. Some of the groups became agricultural collectives (Ein Harod, Tel Yosef, Ramat Rahel). Eventually a more Marxist wing, which felt that class struggle required that the center of gravity shift to the towns, split away from the Histadrut and disassociated itself from Zionism, feeling World Revolution to be more important. This minority faction dissolved in 1928.[32]

Triggering the shift of Jewish political power from the North to the coastal plain was the creation of the Yishuv's three most important institutions: in 1919, the United Labor Party, Achdut HaAvoda (the merger of Poalei Zion and Zeire Zion); the Histadrut in 1920; and the Hagana in the same year. Ahdut HaAvoda's founding conference was in Petach Tikva, and the first convention of the Histadrut in Haifa, but the operating centers were established in Tel Aviv, as well as the locale for the Ahdut HaAvoda newspaper.

The merger of the ideology of the North and the population and economic base of the coastal plain was exemplified in the process of the creation of the Hagana. On June 20, 1920, a conference of workers held at Kibbutz Kinneret in the North called for its establishment as a popular defense mechanism. Then in December, the founding convention of the Histadrut charged a steering committee with creating such a self-defense organization, in place of the more narrowly-base Hashomer. The Hagana remained, in fact, a department of the Histadrut until 1929 when it was broadened to include non-labor interests. Then the National High Command was organized on national representative lines, composed equally of Histadrut representatives and a Citizens' Union (the latter a combination of the Tel Aviv municipality and the Farmers' Association). Both this National High Command and the Hagana, General Staff and Headquarters, were located in Tel Aviv, as was the Histadrut. Other important Tel Aviv-based institutions established during this period were the first Jewish Police Force (1921) and the first Jewish Electric Company (1923).

The large scale immigration waves of the 1920s and 1930s, especially the Fourth Aliya of 1924-1928 from Poland and the Fifth Aliya of 1932-1935, brought overwhelming concentration of population and economic activity to the coastal plain, at its central portion, Tel Aviv. Tel Aviv became the country's largest city, eclipsing Jerusalem, with a population of 135,000 by 1935. Industry grew with great rapidity, especially from 1933-1935. These were years of great prosperity for Palestine, with foreign trade increasing by 50%, over the previous base. The Manufacturers' Association of Palestine, the Stock Exchange, and, in 1939, the Jewish Agency's Economic Council operated from the Tel Aviv base, side-by-side with the powerful Labor Federation's political, economic, and financial institutions.

As the political core clearly became rooted around Tel Aviv, control of its political destinies was more firmly gathered up by the leaders of the Second and Third pioneering immigration waves. The ruling élite included many who retained formal membership in the northern communal and cooperative settlements where they had worked. They brought their central concerns for agricultural pioneering and the development of a national Jewish infrastructure (roads, buildings, ports) to the forefront of the Yishuv's national values. Establishment in 1930 of the powerful United Labor Party, Mapai, a merger of Ahdut HaAvoda and HaPoel Hatzair, aided the process. Mapai succeeded in enlisting many immigrants whose class origins were those of the petty bourgeoisie (highly characteristic of the Polish immigrants of the Fourth Aliya), and the business and professional classes of the Fifth Aliya. The Labor Party's primacy in Palestine made it the single largest and dominant faction in the World Zionist Organization in 1933 with 44% of the vote. This enabled Labor to direct the allocation of World Zionist resources to the fulfillment of Labor's goals in Palestine.

Emphasis on agricultural pioneering during the 1930s shifted from the North to a new area on the coastal plain near Tel Aviv. This was the Sharon Plain and the adjoining Menashe Hill region. Nearby Haifa Bay lands were also heavily settled during this period. Many German and other Central European pioneering groups were involved in this effort. Their settlements provided a physical-ideological "bridge" between the coastal plain core and the North, and the Sharon plain became part of the core area.

The role of the North as embodiment of the Zionist core was to re-emerge in World War II Jewish strategic planning. When Axis military successes in North Africa threatened the British base in Palestine, the possibilities of an allied evacuation placed the Yishuv in great danger. For such an eventuality the Hagana developed a plan to make a folk-fortress of the Upper and Lower Galilee.[33] The Jewish population was to be assembled in the North for a last stand fight. It was felt that the region, with its southern borders in the Valley of Jezreel, the hills of Menashe and Mount Carmel, was defensible. The terrain was well suited to anti-tank warfare, and had airfields and the Haifa port as a lifeline to the outside. Defeat of the Afrika Corps dispelled the danger and the Hagana's strategic plan remained of historic interest only.

From statehood until 1967, the coastal plain, now known as "The Center," increasingly built up its primacy. This was in spite of vigorous governmental efforts to disperse population and economic activities throughout the periphery. But with the Ben Gurion philosophy of Mamlachtiut (state building), the primacy of the state over other institutions tended to centralize matters within the core more than ever. This was especially the case because institutions like the Defense Ministry, the headquarters of the Israeli Armed Forces and the Histradrut did not move to Jerusalem when it became Israel's capital.

JERUSALEM AS A NEW COMPETING CORE

Since 1967, the primacy of the coastal plain core has been challenged by a number of factors. First, unification of Jerusalem and unprecedented growth and development there has shifted a good deal of the national political energy to this upland capital. Jerusalem, the major Jewish urban center until the twentieth century, and a city that had become part of the periphery from 1949 to 1967, began to reassert its traditional role. Jerusalem had given way to Tel Aviv as the largest urban center in the early 1930s, but in 1976, Jerusalem reestablished itself as Israel's single largest city, outstripping the Tel Aviv municipality that has been losing population steadily to its suburbs. Greater Tel Aviv is still three times as populous as Jerusalem, since Jerusalem has almost no urbanized suburbs, while Tel Aviv is largely metropolitan.

It is premature to suggest that Israel's political core is shifting to Jerusalem. However, not only has Jerusalem grown in size and attracted much of the national energy, it has come to symbolize the espousal of particular values by large sectors of the national population. These are new/old values. They have to do with settlement and defense policies, with the issue of frontiers and territorial annexation, and with general attitudes towards the return of the occupied territories.

If Jerusalem is not the political core, it is also no longer the periphery of the state. Jerusalem is now more central to the Periphery than is Tel Aviv. Tiberias in the Upper Jordan Valley via the Bika is two and one-half hours driving distance; Beersheba and Tel Aviv are one hour's drive away; Haifa one and one-half hours journey; and Eilat five hours drive. All of these points have excellent bus and jitney service to Jerusalem. People who live and work in Jerusalem, unlike Greater Tel Aviv's inhabitants, must grapple with the issues of conflict and accommodation with the Palestinian Arabs on a day-to-day-basis. As frontier city inhabitants, Jerusalemites have concerns similar to those settlers living in the North, the Golan and the Northwest Negev — North Sinai. Lines are hardening in Israel between "doves" and "hawks" over the issue of the return of occupied territories. The strength of the doves is in the Tel Aviv area, largely in the Labor Party and in factions and parties to the Left. Doves are led by those whose power base is the Tel Aviv metropolitan Labor Party machinery, allied with intellectual groups and left-wing Mapam kibbutzim. Current labor governmental leadership is somewhere in the middle, caught between the doves and the hawkish ultra-nationalist business and "lumpenproletariat" forces, religious elements and nationalist kibbutz pressures.

Changing Values in the Center

Values within the Tel Aviv core are changing. Until the 1950s they were strongly influenced by the pragmatism of the socialist leadership. Many of these leaders had experienced the pioneering of the North, where defense, settlement and agricultural concerns were paramount; they were prepared for political compromise with the Arabs to preserve gains already achieved. A combination of militancy and compromise, then, characterized this pragmatism.

Not all of labor was unified on this point; in 1944, the Sia Bet opposition group within Mapai split off from the Labor Party, establishing Achdut Avoda, because of its opposition to partition. The core of the Achdut Avoda party was Kibbutz HaMeuchad, then the largest and most militant of the kibbutz movements. For a long time Sia Bet had felt that the Tel Aviv center was no longer according priority to the kibbutz movement, and the partition issue was seen as a weakening of the historic Zionist obligation to settle the land. Another issue was Sia Bet's leaning towards the Soviet Union. Mapai leadership based its political orientation and hopes for statehood through partition on ties with Great Britain and the United States. Helped by its control over the Histadrut, Mapai made partition Labor's policy. Having gained political ascendancy in the core through the weight of its large industrial labor membership, Labor then overcame the opposition to partition by the right-wing ultra-nationalist movement. Their strength lay overwhelmingly in the coastal plain and in the private farm towns, many of which were rapidly becoming urbanized.

Since 1967, issues of security have lost their day-to-day currency for many of the Center's inhabitants. Israeli military control of the West Bank has eliminated the bases of Arab guerilla activity that placed the narrow coastal plain in constant danger. The confrontation line is now remote from Tel Aviv. In keeping with its historic pragmatic attitude, the labor movement within the core, backed by leftist kibbutz representatives in the Periphery, seems prepared for compromise on the question of the return of the territories.

Analysis of attitudes and behavior of the Eighth Knesset members reveals significant differences on the question of the Administered Territories between Laborites living in the Center and those living in or identified with the Periphery.[34] In the Center, 30% can be classified as dovish (they would agree, in exchange for peace, to complete withdrawal save, for most, from East Jerusalem); 55% would settle for the Allon Plan; and only 15% are hawkish. In the Periphery, only 19% of the Laborites are dovish; 57% hold to some version of the Allon Plan; and 24% are hawkish. The picture in Jerusalem is mixed: 22% are dovish; 67% would accept the Allon Plan; and 11% are hawkish.

The right wing Likkud is, of course, the hawkish party. Significantly, however, five of the six Likkud members of the Knesset identified with the Periphery are extreme hawks, while only 52% of its members from the Center fall into this category. Some 34% of Likkud members in the Center are "hawklets", and 14% are likely to opt for a form of the Allon Plan.

For the smaller religious parties, which like the Likkud have no doves, the same distinction between Center and Periphery holds. Nearly all of the Religious Parties' representatives who live in the Center would accept the Allon Plan, but half of those identified with the Periphery are hawks, as are 40% of the Jerusalemites. The dovish parties (Citizen's Rights, Free Liberals, Moked) have their base in the Center and Haifa as do, essentially, the Moderate Free Liberals.

In contrast to the Likkud, 80% of whose Knesset members come from the Center, only 40% of Labor's members of the Knesset come from the Center (the figure for the Religious Parties is 35%). Thus Labor, split within its own ranks over the issue of the territories, is experiencing increasing difficulty in adopting a clear national policy. No longer dominant in the Center, where the opposition Likkud takes a clearly hawkish position, and pressed by its own hawks in the Periphery, Labor has lost its ability to forge a policy that will prevail in the Center and then flow outward to the Periphery.

Changing Values in Jerusalem

With the Periphery adopting a hawkish stand and the Center split, there exists the possibility for Jerusalem to become an ideological rallying point either for those opposed to territorial compromise or for those who would seek it. In effect, Jerusalem may emerge as a second and competing core area to the Center, with its political concerns focusing on Arab-Israeli relations much more than on domestic ideological issues.

During the 1947-48 war, Jerusalem delegates to the Provisional State Council acted as a bloc, pressuring the Government in both the military and international political spheres. Since that time, while there are significant numbers of Jerusalemites in the Knesset (mainly from Labor and the Religious Parties), bloc behavior has disappeared. Instead, the role of the National Parties overrides local considerations. On the whole, Jerusalemite Knesset members from all parties now support the Allon Plan (over half do so, while 30% take a hawkish position, and 20% a dovish stand).

In an electoral system based upon districts, regional bloc politics would become salient. Certain forces would work towards making the Jerusalem bloc more hawkish: it is the city with the largest population of religious and Oriental Jews (backbone of the right-wing and religious parties); it has a strong determination to remain unified; it maintains a frontier psychology that values pioneering (at least in an urban context); it possesses excellent access to Jewish settlement areas of the Periphery.

There are, of course, ideological counter-forces that cannot be ignored. Jerusalem has a vibrant intellectual community with strong tendencies to seek territorial compromise. And it also has a charismatic leader, Mayor Teddy Kollek, a pragmatist of the old school (he initially helped to found a pioneering settlement in the North and rose to prominence as a disciple of Ben Gurion), who is dedicated to finding a modus vivendi with the Arabs of Jerusalem. Many Jerusalemites oppose expansion of Jewish settlement in Samaria, because such a policy may draw energies away from Jerusalem.

Ultimately, however, new local political leadership has to emerge. Such leadership may be less inclined to seek a compromise on territorial issues outside of Jerusalem if it feels it necessary to forge an alliance with the Periphery to protect Jerusalem's unity. This, coupled with the strength of a constantly expanding religious and nationalist lumpenproletarian population within the city (these segments of the populace experience the highest Jewish birthrates), and the bitter memories of Jerusalem's wars and partition, would strengthen Jerusalem's position as a distinct political core. Such an emergence would be an example of a "derived" core — i.e., an area initially built up by energies from the national core which acquires enough strength from internal forces and ties to the Periphery to take on an independent existence.

Policy Implications

Related to Jerusalem's future as a competing core, then, is what may happen within the Periphery to strengthen local forces. This has to do with reform of Israeli electoral law to develop electoral districts. At present, national elections are organized through highly centralized, nationwide party slates. These give disproportionate weight to party bureaucratic leadership in the core and in the pioneering sector. Electoral districts have been postulated as a device to make government more representative. If electoral districting should be enacted, development towns in the Periphery would in all likelihood achieve stronger parliamentary representation. The old links between the pioneering Periphery and Tel Aviv core would thus be further weakened. The development towns in the Periphery exposed to frontier dangers and heavily populated by Jews of Arab-country origin could be expected to take a hard line on the issue of the occupied territories.[35]

In addition, even within the highly centralized collective and cooperative settlement movements, there seems to be emerging a strong, grass-roots force that espouses a folk-level, rather than national level ideology. This process is likely to lead to greater regional unity, linking the pioneering settlements of the outer regions to the development towns. A Golan-Hule bloc is emerging, for example, that exercises strong pressure against territorial compromise. While there are divisions within the various pioneering movements over the issue of settlement of the occupied territories, in the frontier parts of the Periphery, the stand is more strongly hawkish. With the weakening of the leverage of a centralized party, the alliance between the development towns and the settlement movements could bring about a strong common front in the Periphery against compromise.

As stated, the traditional alliance between Israel's Coastal Core and the Periphery is disintegrating, and Jerusalem is emerging as a competing upland core area that strongly identifies with a more independent and egocentric Periphery. Physical and cultural environmental qualities continue to influence policy makers and the pressure groups to which the élite is responsive. To live in the Periphery or in Jerusalem is to be especially sensitive to water resources, to land for agricultural expansion, to space for defensive depth, to topographical features for security, to safe communication lines, and to the value of communalism. Sparcity of population in much of the Periphery, physical and psychological sense of isolation, and face-to-face contact with Arab populations both within Israel and across the "green line", also makes its mark upon attitudes and objectives. This becomes translated into an ideological basis for formulating national policy.

Within the Coastal Core, other forces are at work: the lesser day-to-day concerns with security; the strong sense of being a Jewish majority; the pressures of socio-economic inequality that are more characteristic of Israel's urban life than they are of its rural life; the weaker sense of communalism; and the remoteness of primary resources.

To oversimplify, if Israel's hawks see land or space as assuring security, and Israel's doves seek safety in having a Jewish majority within a more constricted territory, then the distinction between values that develops within the environment of the Periphery and the environment of the Coastal Core comes more sharply into focus. For now, the Coastal Core continues to dominate. But as the gap between it and the Periphery widens, and as the competing Jerusalem Core evolves, with potentially closer links to the Periphery, national consensus will become more difficult to attain.

The major implication of the foregoing is that Israel's abilities to negotiate on the territorial question may lessen, rather than increase with time. There is one countervailing force that could and should be put into play. A politically unified Jerusalem that no longer fears repartition and that develops functional political administrative links with the Arabs of its metropolitan and city-regional areas, is far less likely to become the rallying point for extreme nationalism. For this to occur, however, the solution to the Jerusalem problem cannot await overall Arab-Israeli agreement. Instead, steps should be taken now, through geopolitical restructuring, to insure that Jerusalem, as a competing political core, can show the way to peace through compromise and accommodation.

CORE AND OUTER BOUNDARIES

In the decade that Jerusalem has emerged as Israel's competing core, the major Coastal Plain Core has also expanded (see Figure 11). In the north, Hadera has grown rapidly; in the southeast, Ramleh has developed as Israel's major aircraft manufacturing center; to the south, the new industrial port of Ashdod and the adjoining residential center of Ashkelon have extended the Center's limits.

Population density in the Center averages 500 persons per square kilometer, with more than ten times this density in the Tel Aviv district. Israel's future population will be reflected in continued expansion of the Core, given the population's projected increase from three and one-half million to five million over the next two decades. In all likelihood, the Center will link up with Jerusalem via Ramleh, Emek Ayyalon, Bet Shemesh and the Jerusalem Corridor. The Jerusalem District's population density is already over 500 persons per square kilometer, or the average for the Center. In the north, prospects are for the Haifa districts, whose density, too, is over 500 persons per square kilometer, to be joined to the Core via two corridors, the narrow Coastal Plain and Wadi Milkh. Northeast from Hadera, expansion will embrace the Vale of Irron (Wadi Ara), the Corridor that connects the Coastal Plain to the Valley of Jezreel.

The direction of the southward extension of the Core is more speculative. But with continued growth of Beersheba, and initiation of Yamit as an urban center, the Core will probably envelop the Gaza Strip, extending from Ashkelon southeast to Beersheba and then west to the Mediterranean to include the Rafia Approaches. The latter, the Israeli wedge between the Gaza Strip and the Sinai, is a region currently being developed by agriculture and tourism. The projected development of an Israeli deep-water port at Yamit would provide a major magnet for extension of the Core area to include the Rafia Approaches.

Prospect of the Center's expansion has significant implications for any lasting partition, for the location of the Core sets limits on Israel's political and strategic abilities to compromise on its outer, national boundaries. A unified Jerusalem and the Rafia Approaches that are becoming part of the Core are not likely to be relinquished through diplomatic processes. Moreover, where the Israeli Core adjoins the West Bank and Gaza, lack of periphery to provide defensive depth makes demilitarization of any Arab en-

Fig. 11. Projected Growth of Israel's Political Cores

tity that might emerge a sine qua non for Israel. The Upper Jordan Valley, although in the Israeli Periphery, is also part of the country's nuclear Core. The area, therefore, has greater political influence upon the government than would normally be expected of a peripheral area. Because of this, Israel is at a minimum, likely to insist upon demilitarization of the western half of the Golan Heights in any ultimate formal accommodation with Syria.

Territorial development of Israel's Core and changing configurations of its outer boundaries have made a strong impact upon the West Bank's potential for territorial cohesiveness. Israeli Jerusalem separates Samaria from Judea, and Israel's Negev and Southern Coastal Plain isolates Gaza. Any emerging Palestinian West Bank entity would be truncated, organized around three isolated "corelets" — the Nablus district, the Hebron district and the northern end of the Gaza strip. Israeli objections to emergence of an independent Palestinian West Bank state (Israeli leaders often refer to it as a "rump" state) speak to a lack of viability. Absence of a strong Palestinian Arab core area in the West Bank is certainly a major liability for separate statehood. Under normalized political conditions, the size and dynamism of Greater Amman would make it the logical core area for a combined Jordanian-West Bank state. But Israel is not likely to jeopardize its security by foregoing demilitarization of the West Bank. Moreover, a sovereign Jordanian-Palestinian (or Palestinian-Jordanian) entity can hardly be expected to agree to demilitarization of a major part of its national territory. As an interim measure, therefore, a West Bank entity, truncated, demilitarized and discontiguous (not unlike the European feudal state) is a more logical political option, and Israel could support this entity as a locus for Palestinian self-determination.

FOOTNOTES

1. David Ben Gurion, *Israel – A Personal History, op. cit.,* p. 181. Ben Gurion's statement came in a June 24, 1948 meeting of the Provisional State Council. At this session all Jerusalem members were present and focus of the discussion was whether Jerusalem was part of the Jewish state. Ben Gurion denied that Jerusalem had been discriminated against. He called for attaining military goals *outside* Jerusalem (in the Corridor and through destruction of the Arab Legion in the Triangle) which would secure Jerusalem. He also recommended appointment of a Military Governor.

2. *Ibid.,* p. 178. Rabbi Meir Berlin is quoted by Ben Gurion as saying that he "would not regard it as exaggerated to say that 50 percent of the Jerusalemites would leave if given the opportunity." Dov Joseph noted later that by October 16, 1948, the Jewish Military Government had cancelled 13,400 ration books of persons who had died or left the city. (See Dov Joseph, *The Faithful City, op cit.,* p. 147.)

3. Alfred Lieber, "An Economic History of Jerusalem," in *Jerusalem,* edited by Oesterreicher and Sinai, *op. cit.,* p. 41.

4. The building of these villages in stronghold areas on key hills within the Corridor released regular army units for duty elsewhere. See Dov Joseph, *The Faithful City, op. cit.,* p. 227.

5. Elisha Efrat, "The Hinterland of the New City of Jerusalem and its Economic Geography," *Economic Geography,* Vol. 40, No. 3, 1964, pp. 254-260.

6. Arieh Shachar, "Kavim L'Geographia HaIronit Shel Yerushalayim Ha-Shlema (The Urban Geography of Unified Jerusalem), *"Jerusalem Through the Ages,* (Hebrew), Jerusalem: The Israel Exploration Society, 1968 pp. 145-155.

7. Kimchi et al, *Yerushalayim 1967-1975, Sekira Hevratit Kalkalit, op. cit.,* pp. 92-94.

8. East Jerusalem Census of Population and Housing (1966/67), (Hebrew and English), Jerusalem: Central Bureau of Statistics and Jerusalem Municipality, 1968, 64 pp.

9. Gabriel Padon, "The Divided City: 1948-1967," in *Jerusalem,* edited by Oesterreicher and Sinai, *op. cit.,* pp. 97-99. King Hussein's palace was never completed. The skeleton of its lower stories remains standing to this day.

10. Kimchi et al, *Yerushalayim 1967-1975, Sekira Kalkalit Hevratit, op. cit.,* p. 44.

11. The "Koenig Memorandum", published in the Israeli press in September, 1976, recommended steps to decrease the Arab population of the Galilee by decreasing subsidies to large Arab families, enforcing equal university admission standards for Arabs and Jews (thus, presumably, lessening admission opportunities for Arabs), and encouraging Arab student migration abroad. This Memorandum, drafted by the Interior Ministry's District Representative for the North, was an internal document which, when leaked to the press, evoked a storm of criticism. It has been dismissed by Israeli govern-

mental leaders as irresponsible. On the other hand, it seems clear that the aims of the Memorandum, to decrease the proportion of Arabs in the Galilee, have wide-spread support in Jewish towns of the North.

12. Kimchi et al, *Yerusalayim 1967-1975, Sekira Kalkalit Hevratit, op cit.*, p. 92.

13. *Ibid.*, p. 6.

14. *Ibid.*, pp. 3, 4.

15. Basis for the definition of the metropolitan boundary is the daily commutation shed of Jerusalem, including that of its satellite cities of Ramallah and Bethlehem. In addition, the Jerusalem District is included within the metropolitan area. The author is indebted to Dr. Israel Kimchi, Director of Policy Planning Research, Department of City Planning, Municipality of Jerusalem, for providing a map of his concept of the metropolitan area (the base used is Israel-Administrative Divisions, 1:250,000).

16. Kimchi et al. *Yerushalayim 1967-1975, Sekira Kalkalit Hevratit, op. cit.* pp. 18-19.

17. *Mehoz Yerushalayim, Tachnit Metair Mehozit,* (Hebrew), *(Jerusalem District Outline Scheme),* Jerusalem: Ministry of Interior, Planning Department & the Jerusalem District Planning Office, 1972, (Maps, photographs, texts).

18. *Atlas of Israel,* Jerusalem: Survey of Israel, Ministry of Labour and Amsterdam: Elsevier Publishing Company, 1970, Section IX, Map 11.

19. Amnon Cohen, *Palestine in the 18th Century,* Jerusalem: The Magnes Press, The Hebrew University, 1973, pp. 270-272.

20. *Arthur Ruppin: Memoirs, Diaries, Letters,* edited by Alex Bein (translated from the German by Karen Gershon), Jerusalem: Weidenfeld and Nicolson, 1971, p. 90.

21. The Palestine Mandate was approved by the Council of the League of Nations on July 24, 1922. For full documentation see Great Britain, *Parliamentary Papers, 1922,* cmd. 1785, pp. 1-11.

22. Yehuda Erez, editor, *David Ben Gurion – A Pictorial Record,* Tel Aviv: Ayanot Publishing House, 1953, p. 8.

23. *Arthur Ruppin: Memoirs, Diaries, Letters, op. cit.,* pp. 137-38.

24. Yehuda Wallach, *Atlas Karta L'Toldot Eretz Yisrael Mireishit HaHityashvut V'Ad Kom HaMedinah, op. cit.,* p. 28.

25. This is a quotation from a memorandum presented by David Ben Gurion to the British Labor Party on behalf of the World Poalei Zion. See David Ben Gurion, *Zichronot (Memories),* (Hebrew), Vol. I, Tel Aviv: Am Oved, 1973, p. 164.

26. Colonel Richard Meinertzhagen, *Middle East Diary, 1917-1956, op. cit.,* pp. 61-63.

27. Arthur Ruppin: *Memoirs, Diaries, Letters, op. cit.,* pp. 101-105.

28. Yigal Allon, *Shield of David, op. cit.,* pp. 17-31.

29. Yehuda Wallach, *Atlas Karta, op. cit.,* p. 42.

30. Walter Laqueur, *A History of Zionism,* New York: Holt, Rinehart and Winston, 1972, pp. 75-83.

31. Yigal Allon, *Shield of David, op. cit.,* pp. 70-72.

32. Walter Laqueur, *A History of Zionism, op. cit.,* pp. 295-297.

33. Yehuda Wallach, *Atlas Karta, op. cit.,* p. 76.

34. The author is indebted to Drs. Aharon Davidi and Avshalom Shmueli of the
Department of Geography of Tel Aviv University for having developed a
Territorial Attitudinal Profile of the members of the Eighth Knesset, based
on the following categories:

Hawks (1) — Will concede parts of Sinai for a peace agreement.

Hawks (2) ("Hawklings") — will concede areas in Golan and Sinai, and political presence to King Hussein in the West Bank, for peace.

Allon Plan (3) — will gradually accept Allon Plan if Arabs show some evidence of accepting it also, but do not believe that Arabs wish peace.

Allon Plan (4) — will accept Allon Plan under pressure from the United
States without a formal peace.

Doves (5) ("Dovelets") — will withdraw to the 1948 boundaries, except for
East Jerusalem.

Doves (6) — will withdraw immediately to the 1948 lines, including the loss of
East Jerusalem.

In addition, there are a small number of both Arab and Jewish communist
members of the Knesset, who would accept the 1947 boundaries, or even a PLO
plan for a unified state. These have not been included in the analysis.

Party	Periphery			Center (Including Haifa)			Jerusalem		
	Hawks 1&2	Allon Plan 3&4	Doves 5&6	Hawks 1&2	Allon Plan 3&4	Doves 5&6	Hawks 1&2	Allon Plan 3&4	Doves 5&6
	No.(%)	No.(%)	No.(%)	No.(%)	No.(%)	No.(%)	No.(%)	No.(%)	No.(%)
Labor	5(24)	12(57)	4(19)	3(15)	10(55)	6(30)	1(11)	6(67)	2(22)
Likkud	6(100)	—	—	25(86)	4(14)	—	2(100)	—	—
Religious Parties	2(50)	2(50)	—	1(20)	4(80)	—	2(40)	3(60)	—
Free Liberals	—	1(100)	—	—	—	2(100)	—	—	1(100)
Citizen's Rights, Independent Socialists, Moked	—	—	—	—	—	5(100)	—	—	—

The attitudes were assigned to each member (where known) by four different
individuals who are politically knowledgeable about Knesset life. Where
there was divergence, the opinion was averaged. As further cross-validation,
Nurit Kliot of the Haifa University Geography Department was most helpful
in assessing attitudes in terms of four specific policy issues: 1) Settlement in
Kaddum, 2) The Second Sinai Agreement, 3) West Bank Settlement Plans,
and 4) Negotiations with the PLO.

35. The Israeli Knesset is a 120-member uni-cameral parliament. A variety of
proposals have been made to elect a proportion of the members of Parliament
on a district basis. Two proposals made by Knesset Labor Party Committees
call, respectively, for 30 three-member constituencies and 18 five-member
districts, the remainder to be elected from national party lists. Suggestions
for electoral reform by individuals have proposed as few as 14, to 38, to the
maximum of 120 districts — i.e., one district for approximately 30,000 per-

sons (See Avraham Wolfensohn, *Bechirot Elizoriot B'Medinat Yisrael,* (Hebrew), Haifa: HaLevanon, 1968, 94 pp. Waterman believes that 24 five-seat districts would be an optimum plan (See Stanley Waterman, "Electoral Districting Problems in Israel," draft manuscript, 1976, 14 pp.).

In a 24 district plan, the Periphery would have 33% of Knesset membership, Jerusalem 9%, the Haifa region 13%, and the Center 45%. In most other plans, the Periphery would have 25-30%, Jerusalem 10%, Haifa 10-15% and the Center 50%. Whatever the plan, it is not likely that the present *proportion* of Knesset members who are identified with the Periphery (currently 30%), or Jerusalem (currently 12%) would alter appreciably. What would happen is that there would be a change in attitudinal mix, especially of those in the Periphery. Development town representation would increase to well over 20 from the half dozen who currently hold seats. This is because in all of the proposed districts, the percentage of voters in towns of 5,000 or more is nearly 60% or greater. In the Labor Party, leftist and compromise kibbutz members would diminish in strength as town workers increase their representation. The Likkud would acquire an even more hawkish tone, as its strength in the Periphery increases at the expense of its weight in the Center. Within the Center itself, the small dovish parties would probably be eliminated. Net result of such a change in mix would be felt not only quantitatively but qualitatively, for hawkish positions could influence the dynamics of general Knesset debates.

Geopolitical Restructuring and Planning for Integration

The proposals for geopolitical restructuring of Jerusalem that follow in this chapter are based on the premise of the city's continued territorial unity under Israeli sovereignty. Jews, Muslims and Christians have different perspectives on Jerusalem's political status. What distinguishes the Jewish perspective is the inseparability of the local from the national phenomenon. For Jews, the Holy City is the Land. Jerusalem is Israel and Israel is Jerusalem, Zion being the symbol of the land itself.[1] The Talmud Babli written fifteen hundred years ago said: "Jerusalem will not be rebuilt in its entirety till all the children of Israel will be gathered from exile," and Isaiah prophesied, "In the end of time, Jerusalem will spread over the whole of the land of Israel."[2]

For Muslims and Christians, Jerusalem is a city within some broader national or even global framework. At no time in the 13 centuries of Islamic rule was Jerusalem part of, let alone synonymous with a national entity. Usually it was a district center that belonged to a much larger political system. When cited for its central role within Islam, the city is not mentioned as part of a political framework. Rather, it is treated in a religious context as one of four holy cities, the others being Mecca, Medina and Damascus.

For Christianity, too, Jerusalem's areal setting is not national. Even during its one hundred years of life as a Crusader city-state, Jerusalem functioned as a political outlier of Europe. There is, moreover, some debate within Christianity as to the exclusive religious centrality of the Holy City. While the Apostle Paul did hold Jerusalem to be the geographical center of the world and the center of salvation, others in Christianity gave primacy to the Galilee. This latter view holds the Galilee to be the place of eschatological fulfillment and thus the Holy Land, with Jerusalem as the place of rejection.[3]

SHARING POWER

Because the argument is made here that Jerusalem cannot be territorially shared, it does not follow that all elements of political power need to be monopolized by the national sovereignty, or, indeed, by the municipal sovereignty. Political power in Jerusalem can be shared on a variety of levels with a unified national territorial framework far more easily than within a city divided again between two national sovereignties.

Military and strategic considerations provide one rationale for a unified Jerusalem. Sharing of political power must be the new justification for a unified Jerusalem, and the proposed geopolitical integration is based on the philosophy of shared power. The argument that economic efficiency demands a unified approach is not sufficient to override the needs of Jerusalem's minorities for ideological and social self-expression. A need for some form of autonomy is felt especially by the Arabs who live within the city. Similarly, this need is experienced by West Bankers who work, trade and visit in Jerusalem on an almost daily basis; by visitors from the three faiths for whom the city is the focus of pilgrimage; and by all who hold Jerusalem the Eternal as the Celestial City (Jerusalem the Upper).   Neither Jews nor Arabs have been willing to press the case for urban and regional political integration in Jerusalem. But the scale and pace of the events since 1967 have demonstrated to both peoples that there are greater advantages to their living together in one city than in living separately in one city. The issue no longer is how to redivide, but rather how to accommodate the needs and desires of each people within the common urban setting. The price of a major attempt at developing an integrated political structure will include added tensions, but the price of maintaining an imposed governance structure without genuine political integration will more likely lead to conflict.

Those who believe in the geopolitical and spiritual necessities of a unified Jerusalem under Israeli sovereignty, and this author is among them, need to be more sensitive to the price that such unity exacts. The financial, ideological and security costs of nurturing a mixed Jewish-Arab city are far greater than the costs of merely tolerating a mixed city. These are the costs of the economic and social integration of the inhabitants of the city and its regions.

To advance the pace and level of discussion about the need and possibilities for integrating Jerusalem, this volume offers suggestions for a co-political system that is coordinate with the local, regional and national territorial systems. What is proposed is a geopolitical system to link the political process with physical and socio-economic patterns. This can be the basis for developing plans for an integrated Jerusalem that will meet Israeli needs and assure maintenance of an Arab presence in, and Arab access to, the city.

A STRUCTURE OF GEOPOLITICAL INTEGRATION FOR THE CITY

Political experience as well as analogies drawn from the biological and psychological development of an organism suggest that the political unity of a city cannot be divorced from its geopolitical (physical, political and socio-economic) integration within the city as a system. Jerusalem's problems are compounded by the dualism of its system, one the national Israeli, the other the regional Arab-Jewish. Two other systems, the Arab states and the international Christian community, have, as will be discussed in the next chapter, lesser claims for an equal voice in determining the affairs and future of the city. However, claims for extraterritorial status for the Holy Places are of considerable importance to world-wide religions and there is need to satisfy these claims.

Past Schemes

A number of schemes have been put forward for developing a more effectively unified city that could be more responsive to the needs of its Arab populace. These include: a physically-segregated but politically-centralized city; a two tier system of separate Jewish and Arab towns with a metropolitan administration roof organization; a borough system; a unified city with an enclave system (international) offering extraterritorial rights for places and areas that are of special concern to Christians and Muslims. The plan offered by Lord Caradon calls for equal, dual sovereignty in an undivided Jerusalem.[4] It is a plan for sister cities, Arab Jerusalem under Arab sovereignty, and Jewish Jerusalem under Jewish sovereignty with freedom of movement between the two.

In the months immediately following reunification of the city, considerable discussion and ferment took place among Israeli agencies and individuals, with the aim of developing a political structure for the city that could meet the new situation. One approach dealt with various forms of internationalization of the Old City. The most elaborate solution, the Pragai-Herzog Proposal of 1970, called for division of the Old City into three sections:[5] 1) the Muslim section to include the Muslim authority; 2) the Christian to include the two quarters within the Old City and its outskirts that contained Christian Holy Places, to be governed by a World Central Christian authority; and 3) the Jewish Quarter and the Western Wall which would be part of the city of Jerusalem directly controlled by Israel. Both the Muslim and Christian authorities would have measures of independent sovereignty, defined in terms of treaty rights and with postal and coinage privileges. The Muslim and Christian sectors would have formal borough status within the municipality which would remain a united city, the sovereign capital of Israel. In the discussion of this proposal, a major question emerged over the complexity of developing a Christian representative.

A second general approach dealt with the development of a decentralized system based upon boroughs. The concept was raised quite early (July of 1968) by Meron Benvenisti, then Deputy Mayor of the City for East Jerusalem Affairs. In a preliminary memorandum to the Israeli Foreign Office he suggested that boroughs be developed within a metropolitan framework.[6]

The metropolitan boundaries of Jerusalem would be expanded to include the nearby towns of Bethlehem and Beit Jalla. Each of these towns would be organized as a separate borough, both reverting to Jordanian control. Jerusalem would be divided into three boroughs, one Jewish and two Arab, all three under Israeli sovereignty. The Jewish borough would include West Jerusalem, the Jewish Quarter of the Old City, Mount Scopus, the Mount of Olives, Naveh Yakov, Government House and Beit Hanina. One of the two Jerusalem-Arab boroughs would be urban-suburban; the other would be based on rural villages. The metropolis as a whole would be Jewish-controlled since Jews then constituted two-third's of the area's 298,000 population. This would have been proportionally reflected in the composition of the Greater Jerusalem Council. Head of the Council would be the Mayor, responsible for central services and master planning. Each borough would be responsible for local planning, education and local affairs.

This borough idea was rejected, in part on the grounds that it would lead to partition. To do justice to the concept, it must be remembered that the plan was based on the assumption that there would first be a peace with Jordan. When the Benvenisti plan came to light three years later, it evoked a storm of public disapproval among Israelis. Commenting several years later on the plan and the public uproar, Benvenisti described the plan as a "theoretical exercise, written for a time when no one knew when it would come."[7] The constant accusations leveled at him for being "pro-Arab" led him to resign from his East Jerusalem Affairs post after five years of extraordinary service on behalf of both Jews and Arabs, assuming instead the responsibility for Jerusalem's planning within the municipality.

In 1970, Mayor Teddy Kollek suggested to the Israeli government that the municipality be organized along borough lines with the City Council's membership derived from representatives from each borough.[8] The Israeli government again opposed the plan on the grounds that it would lead to partition.

In general, during this period, Jerusalem's Arabs were reluctant to become partners to any new political schemes for Jerusalem. They feared that entering into agreements with Israel would endanger their ties with the Jordanians, whom they expected to regain control of the West Bank. While some Arabs were prepared to accept the notion of two separate municipal councils under one Jerusalem roof organization, they were not prepared to acquiesce to a borough system that would keep them in minority status. Jerusalem's Arabs were not even ready to form an Arab Advisory Council parallel with a unified Municipal Council, that might have provided them with some measure of authority, nor would they establish neighborhood councils or join standing municipal committees. Only sports and certain cultural organizations were organized as mechanisms of Arab-Jewish joint activities.[9]

Borough plans and other suggestions came to naught, partly because a victorious Israel did not feel compelled by the force of external events to take chances in shaking the newly won unity of the city. But the plans suffered from other weaknesses. They did not provide a framework that allowed for sufficient structural diversity. Moreover, they did not offer sufficient decentralization of power at the smallest scale to guard against possible repartition into two communities. Finally, they generally were dependent upon Israel's "Jordan option" as a precondition to their initiation.

The proposal that is offered here for the restructuring of Jerusalem is based on the recognition that Jerusalem is entangled; it is complex. Whatever geopolitical system is devised must take into account: 1) that ultimately a unified city must have the sovereign power to impose freedom of movement and access on all of its parts; 2) that majority groups must be able to dictate the directions of growth and development; and 3) that minority groups must be guaranteed that this growth and development will not destroy their individual identity. Moreover, this proposal does not depend upon prior agreement with either a Palestinian or a Jordanian state. Instead, it is a plan that can be launched under Israeli initiative. If Jerusalem's Arabs refuse to go along with it, nothing is lost for they do not at present participate in the city's government anyway.

Ideas for the restructuring of Jerusalem can benefit from a developmental geopolitical approach. What are the possibilities and desirability of developing a structure that will be differentiated by neighborhoods and communities; specialized — in social and land-use functions; hierarchial — in divisions of power; and integrated — in the flow of people, goods and ideas? Integration need not, and in Jerusalem's case should not, endanger the cultural uniqueness of neighborhoods and communities that physical separation helps to nurture. This applies to settings within as well as between Jews and Arabs. The physical framework for integration requires that small neighborhoods and larger communities of the two peoples be juxtaposed, and that mechanisms be developed to link these separate units. The units should be large enough to maintain their own sense of identity, but would be tied together through functional exchanges (shopping, work, recreation, technical training, etc.) to form a harmonious mosaic.

The Proposed System

In keeping with the need to develop a system for Jerusalem that is politically and territorially symmetrical, the following five-tier geopolitical system is proposed:

1. *State,* the national sovereignty, Israel, which would ultimately be responsible for the security and territorial integrity of Jerusalem. Whatever Arab state emerged on or embraced the West Bank would have guaranteed access to Jerusalem. Jerusalem's Arabs could maintain dual citizenship, or even West Bank citizenship and a special status of Jerusalem citizens with Israeli residence rights and responsibilities.[10]

2. *Kehillot* (Nations — The Jewish and Arab) which would in effect serve to federate the Communities: the Kehillot are not envisaged as having formal status within the Jerusalem municipal chamber. Their representatives would, however, constitute special delegations to the concerned national parliaments and international organizations (World Jewish, Arab and Christian), to secure special support for religious, cultural and educational needs unique to each people.

3. *City Council,* the roof organization, composed of popularly elected delegates from Community (Borough) constituencies, to carry out the necessary central functions. A city-wide elected mayor would provide a check and balance system to the Community-based City Council.

4. *Communities* (Edot) or Boroughs that are larger, made up of perhaps three to ten neighborhoods, which are also politically-defined, and which, in the hierarchial nature of the structure, would have basic control over the Neighborhoods, but share some of this power with them. There may be from 10 to 15 Communities. These would be represented within the Jerusalem municipal chamber by numbers of delegates in proportion to the Com-

munity's share of the total population of Jerusalem.

5. *Neighborhoods* that are small and differentiated (from 500 to 2,500 families), and which are politically-defined (call them wards) within the city's political system. These may be the individual cells of a Jerusalem municipal chamber. Their political function would be essentially that of a "lobby".

What is proposed is a system of shared political power based upon the proposition that full individual equality is the right and the necessity of each Jerusalemite.[11] The two levels most responsible for the day-to-day administration of the city would be the city government and the Communities. The Kehillot would act as political intermediaries between the two. Kehillot would also mediate between the Communities (Boroughs) and the Neighborhoods, in those cases where the Neighborhoods, normally subordinate to the Communities, are located in Communities dominated by the other nation. Finally, they would mediate between city and state — e.g., the Arab nation would help the City Council and Communities implement high school academic curricula that prepare Arab students for matriculation at Jordanian and other Arab state colleges and universities.

Eventually, as Jerusalem becomes a more fully-integrated metropolis, outlying cities (Ramallah, Bethlehem) or new towns built by Arabs might enter as Communities. Also, there is the possibility that specialized Christian settlement could be attracted from the West. This would be the modern version of the Templars from Germany who established farm settlements in what is now Jerusalem, Tel Aviv, Haifa (and the Galilee) more than a century ago. New Christian settlements located in Jerusalem's metropolitan area or even within the municipal borders might be accorded special community status. Yad HaShemona, a small moshav shitufi ten kilometers from the municipal boundary, provides such a model. Founded by Finnish Christians in 1974, in the hills west of Abu Gosh, and having an economic base in tourism, industry and residence, Yad HaShemona could be a forerunner of such settlements. Kehillot might stimulate the development of single-functional authorities within the city-region in those instances where both West Bank and Israeli territories are affected.

There will inevitably be some measure of duplication and overlap in a system of shared power. However, a clear understanding of the relationship of human needs and goals to the functional differentiation of administrative territorial units should make for a viable system. In the unique case of Jerusalem the State can assume responsibility for physical, health and economic security, and for population growth policy, delegating some of these functions directly to the City Council. Police, fire, urban transportation, water, electricity, sewerage, sanitation and roads would be operationally handled by the city, in some instances acting for the State, or for the Kchillot if the region is served on a metropolitan basis. While investment in housing and industry are state functions, their development and maintenance would be overseen by the city. The city would provide centralized land use planning services, and would set environmental quality standards. Finally, the State is responsible for school construction, salaries and curriculum standards.

The Communities can undertake responsibility for hiring educational personnel and directing educational programming, relying upon ideological guidance and fiscal support from the Kehillot, especially when monies beyond the Community tax base are necessary to equalize investment. The Kehillot would muster such support from religious activity revenues or philanthropies, reaching out to the World Jewish and World Arab communities for help. Building permits and enforcement codes that have to do with land use planning, renewal and environmental quality implementation would also be key Community functions. Obviously this would change the process and output of Master Planning. Other Community functions would include parks and recreation. Some Community responsibilities for education could be delegated to Neighborhoods (e.g., pre-school), as could certain cultural, small park and sports activities.

Taxing and fund raising powers might be shared by State, Kehillot, and Communities, and city corporations could operate in the utilities fields, but responsibility for making decisions on how and where to spend tax revenues should reside mainly within the Communities. A politically integrated system that seeks to preserve its differences needs to be highly decentralized, perhaps to a greater extent than can be rationalized by conventional cost-efficient measures applied to city management.

Methods for financing the city would have to be unique. The Israeli taxation system is highly centralized and Jerusalem, like all other Israeli cities, depends upon services provided directly by national ministries and national organizations (e.g., education, housing, police, health, social welfare), or by national revenues distributed to the city to provide municipal services. The notion of charging Kehillot, Communities and the City with tax responsibilities and powers would require that special fiscal status be accorded Jerusalem. If the Communities were to levy their own taxes to supplement State support, these could be derived from the real and personal property base, applied to owners and renters as appropriate. Taxes now levied by the State in this area would be forgiven. Some of the Community's funds would be allocated directly to the Neighborhood.

The Kehillot would continue to receive funds for their activities from existing sources, including the national governments which now shoulder a major burden. But world philanthropic bodies, Jewish, Christian and Muslim, would be called upon to increase their current levels of support. For the Kehillot should have funds available to go beyond narrow support of specific religious institutions and to initiate or supplement community-wide cultural and educational programs. A special "Jerusalem Tax" might be enthusiastically borne by world organizations, such as the Jewish Agency for Israel, a Pan-Arab Jerusalem Foundation, and World Christian bodies.

Finally, a municipal income tax could be levied on all those who live or work in Jerusalem, deducting the amount from what is paid by the taxpayers in national income taxes. For the municipality to operate a number of services which are partly city-regional in nature, an independently controlled tax framework is needed.

To determine the cost-benefit ratio of such a system of administration and finance might make an interesting study in itself. Setting aside inefficiency costs, the issue is clear. Jerusalem is now a very expensive city to develop and operate because of its uniqueness and because its leadership owes a heavy debt to generations past and future in preserving this uniqueness. A Jerusalem at peace would be a less costly city to nurture and administer than a Jerusalem that must meet terror and prepare for war.

The structure offers a flexible system of hierarchy that contains ample mechanisms for maintaining Jerusalem's heterogeneity among and between its Jewish and Arab populations. The five-tiered system has the hierarchical relationships shown in Figure 12, and Table 5 identifies the various functions to be performed by each unit of government.

METROPOLITAN AND CITY-REGIONAL INTERACTION

In contrast to the holistic five-tier structure that has been pro-posed for the city of Jerusalem, a particularistic approach is sug-gested for its metropolis and city-region. This is because the geo-political framework for the city is built upon undivided (Israeli) sovereignty. However, the broader region is conceived as being ultimately divided between two different sovereignties, Israeli and Arab. The Arab sovereignty is envisaged as Palestinian, al-though it could be Jordanian. Even now there is division of sover-eignty. The Arab sectors are under Israeli military administra-tion, while Jerusalem and the Jerusalem District are an or-ganic part of Israel.

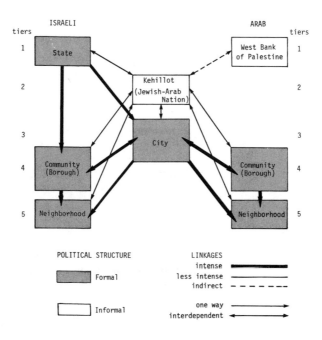

Fig. 12. Five-Tier Governmental Structure for Jerusalem

Table 5

Jerusalem's Five-Tier Governmental Structure

Unit of Governance	*Functions*
State	Physical security (army, police); Social security; Hospitals and other health facilities; Labor exchanges and unemployment benefits; Financing of housing, industrial plants, utilities and transportation infrastructure; School construction, salaries and national curriculum standards
Kehillot (Nations)	Ideological guidance in education, cultural and religious matters
City Council	Operation of fire, transport, water, electric, sanitation and sewerage companies; Constabulary; Road construction and maintenance; Developing and maintaining public housing and markets; Centralized land use planning services; Setting environmental quality standards
Communities (Boroughs)	Building permits and enforcement of land use and environmental quality codes; School personnel administration and hiring, and educational program direction; Operation of parks and recreational programs
Neighborhoods	Pre-school education; cultural, youth and sports activities; small parks

Source of Revenue	*Structure of Government*
National taxation system	Israel parliament appointed sub-committee on Jerusalem
Religious institutional taxes; National and world philanthropic bodies	Citizen-bodies, appointed by city as special delegations to national parliaments and world organizations
State support	Popularly-elected municipal council, weighted by size of Communities; City-wide election of mayor
State support and community-levied real estate taxes	Direct elections within Community
Community support	Administrative wards

Steps to implement a particularistic approach in situations of divided or ambiguous sovereignty can be initiated before resolution of the sovereignty issue. Past discussion of regionalization failed in part because of the non-existence of an Arab sovereignty with which to come to agreement. What is proposed here does not depend upon Arab sovereignty. It puts step-by-step planning first and grants powers to Jerusalem's Arab citizens without demanding a political quid pro quo. Certainly the process of political sharing and planning for interaction can start with Israeli initiative.

Metropolitan Functional Authorities

Metropolitan Jerusalem can be more effectively integrated through establishment of functional administrative entities (See Figure 8). These could be cooperatively planned, supervised and staffed as public metropolitan-wide authorities, or as private companies licensed by groups of municipalities to operate within their political limits. Thus, 1) a Metropolitan Transportation Authority could plan the routes and license jitnies among points in the suburban areas, and between these points and the city. It could also supervise the licensing of Egged (the Israeli bus cooperative) and an Arab bus company; 2) a Solid Waste Disposal and Sewerage Authority could improve public health immediately and forestall long-range environmental problems; 3) a Metropolitan Electric and Water Supply Company could speed development in more backward rural areas; 4) recreation, forest and park areas, camping grounds and multiple-use reservoirs (supplementary water storage, swimming and fishing) could be more effectively used if organized within a metropolitan authority. For example, Solomon's pools might be restored under such a body as a recreational and tourist attraction; 5) a Metropolitan Highway Authority could direct road construction in a way that would better serve local interests; 6) a Metropolitan Urban Housing Estate Authority could provide for planning and environmental impact analysis of housing estates in the suburban villages and towns, including some owned or managed by the Jerusalem municipality; 7) metropolitan market(s) replacing the existing city markets could provide opportunities for wholesale and retail outlets for new metropolitan producer cooperatives. An optimum location for such a new market could be tied into the proposed Jerusalem ring road system, and the existing north-south Nablus-Hebron highway. Markets at Shuafat in the north and/or at Abu Tor in the south might be able to take advantage of transportation and parking infrastructures developed for other purposes as well (e.g., the proposed stadium at Shuafat).

Support for the various metropolitan activities could be derived from direct revenues and national taxes. A Metropolitan Development Council, composed of the city and the metropolitan town and villages could serve as a catalyst. Its primary role would be to initiate the establishment of the individual authorities which would have control over their own operation and funding, responsible to the Council only for renewal of their authorization. The Council would also serve in an advisory capacity to the national government(s) from whom supplementary support is sought. Because the concept of overall metropolitan government is premature and would in all likelihood be unworkable if two national entities were eventually to be involved, it is important to shape the Council as a non-political entity. Thus, the Council would not have fund-generating or fund-allocating powers either through taxation or through levies on participating municipalities. Such leverage would involve it more directly in the political arena than is desirable. In effect, the proposal is for *functional metropolitanization,* with each special purpose district responsible for negotiating its own funding.

City-Regional Bodies

The Jerusalem city-region is envisaged as a combination of the current Jerusalem District and an adjoining Palestinian Arab one (See Figure 9). The Jerusalem District extends from Latrun, Nahshon, Tel Shachar and Tirosh in the west, to Maalot HaHamisha in the north, to Zur Hadassah and Adullam in the south, and to Jerusalem in the east. It is organized as a planning unit of the Ministry of Interior. Were the West Bank to develop a similar district, to include the present Ramallah, Jericho, Bethlehem and Hebron districts, the interests of more effective regional planning would be served. The region's boundaries would be essentially those of the Palestine Mandate's Jerusalem Planning District. This Arab city-region would extend from Dhahiriya in the southwest, to Lubba in the northwest, to Kafr Malik in the northeast, to Jericho, to the eastern edge of the Judean Desert. Such a combined city-region would be a potentially powerful instrument for furthering functional cooperation between Israel and a West Bank entity in other fields of endeavour.

Jointly, the two regional districts could expand on the kinds of planning efforts already being developed by the Jerusalem Planning District: transportation, recreation, tourism, agriculture, settlement and industrial development. Shared management of some activities would help to unify the region without detracting from independent, national considerations. Perhaps the most immediate need is to establish a joint labor exchange to rationalize and supervise the flow of labor, especially Arab labor, into Jerusalem, into some of the surrounding agricultural settlements, and into the regional service infrastructure.

Development and management of industrial estates would be an appropriate joint activity for a specially created industrial authority in those cases where the labor supply is strongly mixed Arab-Jewish. Perhaps most immediate on the agenda of city-regional needs are bodies that will coordinate water planning (consumption, agricultural irrigation and drainage), and expand Judean Hills forest development so that it will not be distorted by national boundaries. For example, a new national park is under development in the high hills of the southern section of Israel's Jerusalem district, extending from the southwest border of the city and including the villages of Mevo Betar, Bar Giora, Nes Harim, Mata and Mahasiya. This park, known as the American Bicentennial Park, involves the replanning and redevelopment of the five hill villages to provide them with a more stable economic base. The area includes only the Nahal Soreq watershed within Israeli territory. South of the "green line", from Battir to Wadi Furkin, are Arab areas which drain into Emek Haela, the basin south of the Soreq Basin. Their inclusion would enhance the general development plan. As with the proposal for separate metropolitan authorities, the city-regional bodies would be organized functionally as separate bodies. Perhaps, ultimately, these atomized organizations would feel impelled to seek mechanisms to coordinate their diverse activities. However, this should be left to the future, when the politics of two national sovereignties permit such coordination.

ACTION SPACES FOR GEOPOLITICAL INTEGRATION

Social scientists generally promote the proposition that spatial integration enhances social interaction, leading eventually to decreased levels of tension and conflict between groups.[12] On the other hand, some real-life experiences of inter-group conflict seem to suggest the contrary: in Northern Ireland where the two religious communities clash across a common street boundary; in the United States where racial groups integrated within public housing projects or schools live in the midst of turmoil and violence; in Cyprus where the two ethnic communities lived in bordering city quarters in a state of constant siege or war. In the face of such a record, it is clear that spatial integration is not in and of itself a basis for positive social interaction. For geographical propinquity as an independent variable to have a conflict-reducing role, there must be some element of socio-cultural or economic-functional symmetry between the contending groups.

Arabs and Jews hold opposing religious, cultural and political traditions and aspirations. To use spatial integration as a mechanism for bridging some of these differences — i.e., via the same place of worship, the same dwelling unit or the same political clubhouse — would be to invite failure. In Israel, differences among Jews that are less deep-rooted than between Jews and Arabs have been exacerbated by spatial integration. Attempts in the 1950s to mix Oriental and Eastern European Jews in cooperative settlements often failed, and recent efforts to integrate Georgian and Westernized Jews within the same apartment dwelling or block are creating major social tensions.

The case for spatial integration in Jerusalem as well as elsewhere in settings of deep-seated conflict must therefore rest upon efforts that do not threaten the socio-cultural raison d'etre of the concerned groups. The problem for planning is to facilitate peoples' getting to know each other better, without their losing their anchor points.

Groups that are encouraged to live in adjoining quarters should have as similar a set of class and economic interests as possible. This holds to a lesser extent for those expected to study side-by-side in schools or in libraries. Where interaction focuses on health care, recreation, transportation, work or commerce, there are far greater opportunities for mixing the two peoples, irrespective of class or cultural traditions.

Thus far in Jerusalem, neither politics nor planning for the city's growth and development has been centrally concerned with spatially interactive processes. Instead, the concern has been with promoting the Israeli presence in the eastern sector. Of

course the reasons for this state of affairs are complex. They include not merely Israeli egocentrism but also Arab reluctance or
unwillingness to participate publicly in formal partnership with
Jews in guiding Jerusalem's growth and development. The Arabs
of Jerusalem are not free agents. They must guide themselves in
their behavior towards Jews in the context of the unfolding
events of the Arab-Israeli conflict.

Planning that now is or will be undertaken to embrace Arab
development of Jerusalem will have to be conducted largely by
Israeli bodies. What is suggested to the Arabs may well be rejected. To plan for Arab-Jewish interaction in Jerusalem is not to
guarantee that such interaction will take place. But without
planning for interaction that will have some geopolitical consequences, there is even less promise of developing a political dialogue between the two Kehillot.

Past Experience

This is not to imply that there has not already been some action
taken by local governmental authorities to try to develop facilities to promote Arab-Jewish interaction. Some projects have
been put into operation — a swimming pool, a community center,
a library, a few apartments within a Jewish housing estate.
Others are under construction: a youth wing at the Rockefeller
Museum with studios and classrooms to serve both peoples, and
the Liberty Bell Park at Omariya whose recreation facilities will
be accessible to both Jews and Arabs. Moreover, the Jerusalem
City Council has authorized the Mamilla Urban renewal project
as a "living bridge" between the Old and New Cities and the Arab
and Jewish peoples.

But these are single and sporadic projects. Initiative for them
has come from the mayor of the city and from isolated, interested
individuals, almost exclusively Jewish. Such projects may be
viewed as important efforts to promote Arab-Jewish cooperation.
They are not, however, part of a master scheme for integrating
the city. Without physical and socio-economic contact, systems of
political integration have little chance of enduring. In particular,
any federated system that might one day be imposed upon a geopolitically unintegrated system could be easily dismantled in the
face of external world or Arab pressures.

For interaction space to play a positive political integrational
role, the political system of Jerusalem must be altered to accom-

modate some of the ideological needs of the Arabs. The geopolitical structure that has been proposed in this chapter is aimed
at fulfilling such a purpose. Weingrod and Mendes-Flohr's study
of post 1967 Arab-Jewish relationship in Jerusalem is revealing
for what it has to say about the development of links in a political
system regarded by the Arabs as imposed and coercive, and without any sharing of power.[13] Business or economic interests were
found to be the strongest basis for interaction between Jew and
Arab. Usually the work relationship is hierarchical, with the
Arab in subordinate status. Sometimes Arab and Jewish teams
from the same organization work at separate tasks, either at one
job (e.g., construction), or in different areas (e.g., Arab employees
of the municipality serving Arab sectors).

A second interaction area analyzed was a children's ward in a
hospital. Arab and Jewish children related to each other in normal child play fashion and Arab children quickly were assim-
ilated into the hospital system. Jewish and Arab neighborhoods
that adjoin one another were also studied for their interaction
patterns. Distance, formality and some hostility were the major
characteristic for a neighborhood along the former "green line"
(Abu Tor), but where people lived very close to each other, normal
visiting relationships developed, mostly initiated by women.
Common language (Jews speaking Arabic) and working class ties
stimulated interaction. The Arabs of Beit Safafa (part of which
was in Israel before 1967) and the Jews of the Katamonim inter-
act by shopping in the same local stores, sitting around the same
square (women and children), and mingling at the same medical
clinic. As in Abu Tor, physical proximity and common language
are important in developing more systematic social ties.

The above cited study emphasized that close contact between
the two peoples has little influence on general political outlooks,
and does not lead to mutual political understanding. Indeed such
contacts cannot affect political attitudes as long as there is no
sharing of political power.

Rationale for Planning

There are four geographical convergence zones in Jerusalem
within which exist opportunities and challenges for spatial interaction: 1) inside the Old City; 2) between the Old and New Cities;
3) between East and West Jerusalem, and 4) between Arab and
Israeli settlement in East Jerusalem. These convergence zones lie

along the boundary lines of potential Communities. The development of interaction points between Communities (or Neighborhoods) would help to unify the political structure previously proposed.

Within the Old City, reconstruction of the Jewish Quarter that was destroyed in the fighting of 1947-48 has proceeded rapidly since Jerusalem was united. This includes residences, institutions, shops, inns, and parking. At present, there is very little organized renewal in the Christian, Armenian and Muslim Quarters. Eventually, the plan for Old Jerusalem calls for a thinned down population of 20,000 (the population is now 24,000) including 3,500 Jews and 10,000 Muslims. But implementation of the full plan will doubtless have to await clarification of regional and international political events.

In the interim, the Old City continues to lose some of its middle and upper mercantile classes, especially Christians and Armenians who seek better living conditions outside the walls. Without shared class or social interests between Jews and Arabs, the potential for interaction will remain minimal. Planning of Old Jerusalem has focused on buildings, without much thought to the issue of social interaction. The Jews moving into the Jewish Quarter are mainly religious, but include middle to upper income professionals and government bureaucrats, as well as Yeshiva students. Their Arab neighbors are small shopkeepers and workers, with whom they have little in common. If the "ghettoization" of the Jewish Quarter is to be avoided, a conscious effort must be made to broaden the mix of entering Jews. Small and middle class storekeepers, workers, university students and middle-range municipal employees could provide a mix for interaction. Under such circumstances, the barrier between the Jewish Quarter and the rest of the Walled City would be reduced.

At the inner edge of the Quarter it would then be possible eventually to develop a central market area to house merchants of all communities, in addition to the shops and bazaars that are specific to each quarter. A central business area would encourage more commercial specialization — e.g., restaurants, jewelry, leather, antique, handicraft and specialized food shops, boutiques and smaller numbers of general food and dry goods stores.

In planning for spatial integration elsewhere than in the Old City, it may be useful to suggest some operating principles: 1) that the strongest attachment to local territory (at the block or apartment house scale), and therefore the greatest resistance to physical penetration of neighborhood borders by outsiders, can be expected of highly religious or lower socio-economic class people; 2) that there is great need to concentrate on means of enhancing physical mobility within the entire city, by improving the road, parking and public transportation system. Unless this is done, new housing and industrial development may enhance atomization rather than unification; and 3) that the travel range for jobs, recreation, specialized shopping and advanced schooling should be made deliberately more extensive than the travel range for fulfilling normal residential, and general goods and services needs. By influencing the development of individual travel ranges that vary in their extent according to functions, planners will be able to reduce the general feelings for local territorial autonomy, and, thus, reduce local territorial conflict. Wherever possible, new service and shopping areas should take up border positions that lie between Neighborhoods and Communities, rather than occupy central locations within them.

Spatial integration of the system does not mean uniformity. It does mean greater links among parts in a system that is specialized, hierarchical, and increasingly complex. Scale is one key to successful interaction. There must be a kind of symmetry in size, and to a certain degree, in harmonization of physical and social-economic form between adjoining Neighborhoods and Communities if more than coexistence is to be attained. A Ramot of 5,000 family units has a better chance to seek ways of interacting with a Beit Hanina and Beit Iksa and Shuafat of similar size. Should Ramot of 10,000 units be developed, its adjoining Arab villages would be dwarfed in size and in architectural scale. The same may be said for Giloh's relationship to Beit Safafa. The implications of this are that future development of these two Israeli quarters should follow a far more dispersed pattern. Emphasis should be put on a two-story villa rather than on an eight-story apartment, leaving enough spaces between each section to create a dispersed suburbs scale, rather than following the Bronx-style apartment block model as is the case now. Moreover, planned development for Arab housing in Beit Hanina and Beit Iksa, and in Beit Safafa would help preserve a size balance. Were some of the Jewish housing to take on a suburban quality even to include cooperative villages, like moshavim, but with an industrial, not an agricultural base, there would be a better fit with the Arab rural-suburban surroundings.

Granted that differences between Jews and Arabs are expressed in many different ways — language, religion, dress, family tradition, etc., and that the attendant clash of values cannot generally be mitigated, there are certain cultural differences that have to do with life style that can be bridged by more harmonious residential forms and patterns. The cultural shock experienced by Arabs whose dwellings are located near new Israeli housing estates may be inferred from the photographs that are shown. These are views of the estates taken from within the area (the "near Israeli" view); from a road normally traveled by Israeli passers-by (the "outside" Israeli view); from an Arab house that adjoins the development (the "near Arab" view); and from an Arab village that is within a few hundred meters away (the "outside Arab" view). For the Arab, the Israeli housing estates loom up as fortresses — forbidding, alien elements of landscape (See following section of *Photographic Perspectives*). For the Jews, they are part of the normal Israeli apartment house landscape. Scaling Israeli housing in East Jerusalem more to a form that is in keeping with Arab land use could help to reduce the more general culture clash.

Socio-economic matching of juxtaposed new Jewish and Arab housing estates would further encourage contact. At the working class levels the residential dividing lines should be sharp. At the upper class levels there may be some room for interpenetration (e.g., Arabs living in single story villas next to Jews, on the borders of the estates). To provide for more suburbanized housing styles, it might be necessary to enlarge modestly the present boundaries of the city. The political liabilities of such a step are great. Most Arabs would oppose this as encroachment on West Bank Territory. Many Jews would object as diverting energies from the need to consolidate and expand the Israeli housing estates that have been built in East Jerusalem. Such suburbanization could have the consequence of making both Kehillot more secure because of their mutual vulnerability. Moreover, modest expansion of the city's boundaries could bring additional numbers of Arabs into the population base, strengthening the Arab presence in Jerusalem. Finally, extending the boundaries would enhance Jerusalem's role within the metropolis, reinforcing the link between Israel and the West Bank.

Photographic Perspectives of East Jerusalem's Israeli Housing Estates

(photos by Werner Braun)

in center at Ramat

graph backed by cottages and apartment houses.

3. An "Outside Israeli" view — from helicopter looking at Levi

HaMivtar from street and cottages of Ramat Eshkol.

5. A "Near Arab" view — from house of Bedouin in Arab Es-Sawakra (local site is Mukaber Es-Sawakhra), School of Armon

small cluster). Looming above are Hebrew University dormitories of Mount Scopus.

7. An "Intermediate Arab" view — Bedouin family in their own

looking northward to Armon HaNatziv.

A current controversy among planners and politicians revolves around the issue of how far beyond city limits it is desirable to promote Jewish urban and suburban settlement. Some proposals would establish a development ring or sprawl approximately ten kilometers outward. Opponents, including Jerusalem municipal leaders, criticize this as unrealistic and express the fear that development within Jerusalem's limits would be set back severely. A compromise extension of two to four kilometers in the north and northeast, and in the southwest corner might accommodate some of the Jewish suburbanization that has been suggested here, including the development of industrial moshavim.

Even more important than symmetry in numbers of people, which may no longer be achievable in many situations in Jerusalem, is the location of facilities designed to promote contact and perhaps interdependence. Most such facilities can be located at points of convergence, where members of the two Kehillot live side-by-side. While most areas of interaction potential are in East Jerusalem at convergence points between the new Jewish housing estates and Arab residential areas, some promising points may be found in West Jerusalem, especially at or near the pre-1967 border and in areas that are new or that face urban renewal. These include Mamilla, Musrara, Abu Tor, Katamonin-Beit Safafa-Giloh, American Colony-Sheikh Jarrah-Shmuel HaNavi. Arab laborers already are accustomed to spending their day-hours in West Jerusalem, and tourists can serve as a particular stimulus for Arab activities. In most cases, neutral grounds are suggested, for they have long been recognized as the best meeting places for hostile groups. Examples of potential activity spaces follow (See Figure 13):

Potential Activity Spaces

a. *Shopping* — The proposed urban renewal project for Mamilla is an ideal site for encouraging Arab shops and boutiques to locate side-by-side with Jewish-owned shops. Until 1947, Mamilla was an integrated commercial quarter and its redevelopment plan provides shopping, parking and vehicular access between the Old City and West Jerusalem. Also some planned shopping facilities in the new Jewish housing estates could take up peripheral locations that would lie between the Jewish Quarter and the Arab suburbs, to encourage mixing of

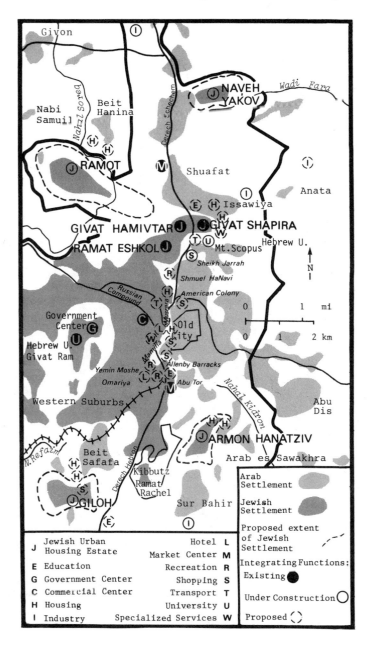

Fig. 13. Foci for Jerusalem's Integration-Activity Spaces

shopkeepers and customers. Essentially, reference is to separately-owned establishments. Jointly-owned enterprises are not ruled out, but they are not likely to develop in significant numbers. A locational key to the success and permanence of such business foci is meeting points of Jewish and Arab neighborhoods, and "central zones" where heavy influxes of foreign visitors or non-Jerusalemite Jews and Arabs congregate or could congregate (e.g., adjoining the gates of Old City — Yemin Moshe, American Colony, Mamilla; north of Sheikh Jarrah on road to Mount Scopus; or between Katamonim and Beit Safafa, and Beit Safafa and Giloh).

Projects designed as "bridges" must take into account Arab architectural and cultural tastes and economic capabilities. The plan for the Mamilla renewal project, conceived as a "living bridge" between the Old City and West Jerusalem, may, by its very cost, its grandiose and modernistic scale, and the 15 to 20 years construction time span, make Arab participation as shopkeepers or residents unfeasible. The plan does call for a pedestrian arcade depressed below the ground. This would follow the present line of Mamilla Road from King David Street in West Jerusalem to the Old City's Jaffa Gate. Shops lining the arcade are conceived as an extension of the Old City Shuk, and parking is to serve Old Jerusalem as well as visitors. Without provision for subsidized rents, for the architectural and service tastes of Arab shopkeepers, and for the agglomerative tendencies of Arab businesses, however, the wanted Arab presence is not likely to be attracted.

b. *Education* — It is almost impossible to conceive of Arab-Jewish integrated schools, not merely on political grounds but also on the basis of what molds community and nation. One exception to this however, is the trade-vocational-technical school (e.g., machinists, electricians, carpenters, draftsmen, construction estimators) which appeals to youths of an age level where culture is less important. There seem to be locational opportunities for such schools: 1) where East and West Jerusalem meet, e.g., Derech Hebron to serve Jewish Giloh, Talpiyot and Geulim, and growing Arab areas in Sur Bahir, Arab Es-Sawakhra and Bethlehem. The new Youth Cultural Educational Wing of the Rockefeller Museum is another example of this location type; 2) where Jewish housing estates impinge upon Arab sections of East Jerusalem, e.g., Derech Schechem between Givat Shapira and Shuafat; and 3) where Jewish sections offer easy access to Arab areas, such as the Allenby Barracks in Jewish Abu Tor that have excellent approaches to Arab villages to the east. Since younger children have prominent roles to play in promoting integration between hostile groups, educational, recreational and sports establishments are especially focal.

c. *Housing* — West Jerusalem appears to offer modest opportunities for developing housing for Arabs. Certainly far more buildings for Arabs can be encouraged by Israeli governmental action in East Jerusalem than have been the case to date, particularly close to, rather than removed from new Jewish housing estates. From 1968 through 1974, 1310 new residential units accommodating 8,000 persons were constructed by Arabs. Nearly all of this housing is private, and removed from axes of Jewish-Arab convergence. It is mostly located within rural villages like Issawiya, Arab Es-Sawakhra, Umm-Tuba, and Sur Bahir, which were incorporated into the municipality after 1967. The very few municipally stimulated apartment building projects for Arabs have been located in Shuafat, adjoining Derech Schechem and in Beit Hanina. Housing convergence points at which public Arab housing might be built include: 1) in East Jerusalem between Beit Safafa and Giloh; between Beit Hanina and Ramot; between Issawiya and Givat Shapira, and 2) in West Jerusalem in East Talpiyot and in renewal areas of Musrara and Mamilla. Reference to the need for housing intervention is not to privately initiated mortgage loans (Israel's Housing Ministry has granted them to 4,000 East Jerusalem Arabs), but to large-scale public building in areas that can share shopping, work and other common facilities with Jewish housing estates.

d. *Hotels* — The possibility for one or more Arab-owned hotels in West Jerusalem seems excellent. In general, Arab-managed hotels in the eastern part of the city provide quality service in modest quarters, a commodity often absent from West Jerusalem. There is an ambiance to an Arab hotel that will appeal to Jewish tourists, especially if located in the western side of the city. Logical new points for Arab hotels purchased or built, would be the Omariya, Musrara, or the Mamilla areas. Arab-owned hotels might serve the further purpose of anchoring Arab specialty shops and restaurants.

e. *Recreation and Entertainment* — Arab night clubs and restaurants have strong appeal not only for tourists but for Israelis. Since they operate on the Sabbath, locating them in West Jerusalem poses considerable difficulties, requiring locations that will not provoke Orthodox Jewish populations. An area such as the railroad station, near or adjoining the Khan night club, would offer a likely site. So would Omariya, where the Liberty Bell Park recreational facilities are underway, and Yemin Moshe and Mamilla, all of which would have easy access to Arab residential areas. Recreation centers for Arabs and Jews could be developed in the Jewish areas west of the American Colony. Also, the new Jerusalem sports stadium that is planned for Shuafat could become the anchor for a recreation complex (swimming pools, tennis courts, youth track and football fields) that would serve both Kehillot.

f. *Professional Services* — The majority of Arab workers in Jewish Jerusalem are construction workers who are spread around the city. Some hold jobs in workshop, factories and garages, which have more specialized locations. There is need to attract the Arab middle class and professionals to areas where there are also Jewish concentrations of such professionals. As a start, buildings to house lawyers, accountants and dentists, Arabs and Jews, who reach out to mixed clientele, might be developed. Mamilla would be a logical spot for this, as would a specialized building near the Hebrew University Mount Scopus medical hospital.

g. *Transportation* — Promoting the common use of buses and taxis can be a useful device for interaction. To this end, more bus routes might be redirected to serving Communities of the two peoples on the same lines. Also, terminals for interurban jitnies and taxis could be located at points of convergence near the gates of the Old City, the northern end of the Russian Compound, or adjacent to Mount Scopus. Because of the sensitivity of both peoples to security problems while riding in buses, the jitney service appears to have a more immediate pay-off as a focus for interaction.

The locational strategy suggested calls for a number of small, widely-distributed interaction activities. The emphasis is on accessibility and wide choice, rather than concentration of multi-functional activities in one area.

WALLS BUT NOT BARRIERS

Jerusalem has been a city of walls since its founding. Some of the walls are made by man, some by nature and still others are in the minds of men. It is not likely not even desirable that these walls will be eliminated. It is hoped, instead, that the psychological heights of the walls will be lowered through the process of integration; that the walls will differentiate peoples and cultures, but not seal them off from one another; and that the walls will promote unity for Jerusalem as a system, not continue to fragment it.

The Four Walls of Jerusalem

Jerusalem is marked off by four concentric walls (See Figure 14, and the following section entitled *Photographic Perspectives of the Four Walls of Jerusalem,* p. 149). The innermost is the wall of the Ancient City, rebuilt by the Sultan Suleiman the Magnificient from 1537 to 1541. The wall has been beautified since reunification with surrounding gardens, lights and parks. It now stands as the city's primary magnet for residents and visitors alike, rather than as the military barrier that it so recently was.

The second ring is the New Jerusalem's wall of hills topped by buildings that surround the city like a diamond.[14] To the east is the ridge of Mount Scopus, the Mount of Olives and its southern extension. Along the skyline of this eastern ridge are large public institutions — the Mount Scopus campus of the Hebrew University, the Hadassah Hospital, Augusta Victoria Hospital, the Intercontinental Hotel. To the north and west are ridges that are part of the main waterdivide of the Judean Mountains which separates the Mediterranean from the Dead Sea drainage. This main ridge runs from French Hill (Givat Shapira) near the junction with Mount Scopus, southwest to Romema, then southeast along King George Street to the King David — Y.M.C.A. junctions, and then southward as the Abu Tor — Ramat Rahel ridge (called Givat Hananya, at the north end of the ridge, and Jebel Mukaber at its highest point, Government House). Along this main ridge is a nearly uninterrupted string of office buildings, apartments and hotels. The heights of the buildings are fairly even save for the high rise projection of the Plaza Hotel in the

Fig. 14. The Four Walls of Jerusalem

west and the Hilton Hotel at the northwest (in Romema). Thus, the second wall is a product of both nature and man.

The third wall, man-made, is still in the making. The wall is not continuous, but consists of the separate massive clusters of modern housing estates that loom over nearby Arab villages and fields. These are, clockwise from the northwest, Ramot, Naveh Yakov, Armon HaNatziv and Giloh. They represent much of the new Jewish presence in the expanded city and are in stark architectural contrast with the surrounding low-lying suburban-rural Arab sprawl.

The fourth wall has been forged by nature. In the west, especially, it consists of the escarpments that overlook deeply incised valleys which mark off the Jerusalem plateau from adjoining uplands. In the southwest, Nahal Refaim and its southeastern tributary carve off the escarpment, dividing the Jerusalem plateau from heights at Beit Jalah and Battir. From the west, Mevasseret Zion, Motza and Lifta are points which look onto the escarpment formed by Nahal Soreq. This same stream farther north forms the escarpment, from the perspective of Beit Iksa and Beit Hanina. In the northeast, Wadis Suweinit and Fara, tributaries of Wadi Qilt, loom up before the villages east of Bira. In the southeast, Nahal Kidron forms a wall against the Judean Desert. In the east, the escarpments run east-west rather than parallel to the city, so that steeply sloping desert badlands rather than a discreet rim serve as the boundary.

Legend has it that the Walls of Jerusalem had special qualities; that whoever gazed on them was cured of his ailments and that ministering angels guarded the walls. "Thou shalt call thy walls Salvation and thy gates Praise."[15] Would that these legends were now to apply to all of Jerusalem's walls! Man must determine whether the walls of Jerusalem are to play the role of good neighbor fences or barriers. The geopolitical restructuring of Jerusalem and the planning process that support human interaction and integration can help to break down the barriers that man and nature have erected. To this end bold political steps need to be taken now — by Israel which has it in its power to take the initiative; by Arabs whose maintenance and strengthening of their position depends upon their receptivity to such initiative; and by outside powers whose endorsement of the unity of the city can encourage the initiative, and support the mechanisms that can lead to the successful development of a co-political community in the Holy City.

Photographic Perspectives of the Four Walls of Jerusalem

(photos by Werner Braun)

1 Innermost Wall — *Damascus Gate leading into the Muslim*

excavations in foreground, overlooked by El Aksa mosque. New buildings of rehabilitated Jewish Quarter are to the left behind the wall, just behind Dung Gate opening.

3. Innermost Wall — *East Wall* of Old City, enclosing Haram esh Sharif, with the Dome of the Rock to the right, and the El Aksa mosque to its left rear. At the base of the wall, extending southward from the Golden Gate, is the Muslim cemetery. Below the cemetery is the Valley of Gethsemane which joins the Valley of Kidron

by Church of the Dormition. Tower at middle of wall is the Citadel, to the left of which is the Jaffa Gate, adjoined by parking lot. In the center of the photograph, and running along the base of the wall, is the Valley of Hinnom.

5. Second Wall — *Mount Scopus* ridge, topped by the Hebrew University. Houses in foreground are in Wadi Joz, Arab Quarter

on the right, the Hebrew University in the center and Augusta Victoria Hospital on the left. View is from the desert in the east, with the Arab village of Isawiya at the base of the ridge.

7. Second Wall — *French Hill* (Givat Shapira) with cottages below and apartment houses along the ridge. View is from the

...Hotel at extreme right, and the tower of Y.M.C.A., on near right. Large building in center is the Plaza Hotel which lies atop the ridge at King George Street. Omaria residential quarter is at far left of photograph.

9. Second Wall — *Abu Tor ridge with housing on its crest. Below*

10. Second Wall — from ridge at *Ramat Rahel*, overlooking Armon HaNatziv housing estate. The wooded ridge to the left rear of apartment blocks is Jebel Mukaber. White buildings amidst the trees is Government House.

11. Third Wall — *Ramot*, the northwestern Israeli housing estate, is in the upper part of the photograph. In the foreground is the Valley of Soreq, with the abandoned Arab village of Lifta to

At *Nabil Wall*, *Naveh Yakov*, the northeastern Israeli housing estate is in the center of the photograph. In the foreground is the Arab village of Anata. Ramallah-Bira on top of ridge at upper left of the photograph lies to the north of Naveh Yakov.

13. Third Wall — *Armon HaNatziv* (East Talpiyot) is the south-

14. **Third Wall** — *Giloh* is the southwestern Israeli housing estate. On top of ridge at upper left are heights of Beit Jala.

15. Fourth Wall — incised stream *Nahal Soreq*, with abandoned Arab village of Lifta at center of slope and Romema Quarter at top escarpment. View is at western edge of city, looking north-

Hotel is at far right. Nestled in on the lower slope of the Valley of Soreq in the right foreground is the residential suburb of Motza.
The forested slope above Motza is Har Menuhot. The road climbing along the valley is an ancient Roman way.

17. Fourth Wall — incised valley of *Nahal Refaim*, through which railroad ascends to Jerusalem. At top of escarpment on

18. **Fourth Wall** —*Judean Desert badlands* that lie east of Jerusalem. View is from Tel Anata with Dead Sea and Moab escarpment in far distance.

19. **Fourth Wall** — *Mount of Offence*, center of photograph, at base of which *Naḥal Kidron* cuts southward into Judean desert. In foreground, Mount Zion on left and Abu Tor ridge on right are bisected by Valley of Hinnom. In distance are Judean desert

...antique Wall Composition — (1) First Wall — South Wall of Old City in center of photograph; (2) Second Wall — Mount Scopus and Givat Shapira, from right to left at top; and (3) Fourth Wall — Kidron Valley, lower right corner, with "City of David" Arab houses to the left of the valley.

FOOTNOTES

1. Davies notes that in the post-exilic period, life of Jewry was mainly centered in Jerusalem and its surroundings, the city becoming the quintessence of the land. He expands on this theme to show how Zion (Jerusalem) later became the center of the world, the symbol of the land itself and the focal point for the Messianic Age. See W.D. Davies, *The Gospel and the Land, op. cit.,* pp. 131-196.

2. As quoted by Zeev Vilnai, *Legends of Jerusalem, op. cit.,* p. 153 *(Babli, Berachot,* 49a), and p. 158 *(Isaiah: 60:8).*

3. W.D. Davies, *The Gospel and the Land, op. cit.,* pp. 198-204, 409-438.

4. Lord Caradon, "The Only Solution," *The Reader's Digest,* March, 1975, pp. 134-135.

5. Uzi Benziman, *Yerushalayim-Ir L'Lo Homa, op cit.,* p. 293. In pp. 282-284, Benziman also discusses a forerunner of the Pragai-Herzog proposal — the Levontin report. This was submitted by Professor Avigdor Levontin to a group of Israeli ministers and other officials one month after the conquest of the Old City. The report called for functional internationalization of the Walled City. The idea was that Israel would retain de jure sovereignty, but would guarantee the status quo with the Old City — i.e., safeguarding the interests of the three faiths and treating the area as a city of historic preservation. International Muslim and Christian Councils would have a special supervisory status over their Holy Places, reporting directly to an Israel Foreign Minister's Office of Religions. The Jewish Quarter and Western Wall would come under the direct supervision of the Israeli state.

6. *Ibid,* pp. 291-292; Norman Gosenfeld, *The Spatial Division of Jerusalem, 1948-1969, op. cit.,* pp. 366-370; *The Jerusalem Post,* April 30, 1971; and Abraham Rabinovich, "Plan for Jerusalem," *The Jerusalem Post,* May 7, 1971.

7. Meron Benvenisti, *Mul HaHoma HaSegura, op. cit.,* p. 327.

8. Uzi Benziman, *Yerushalayim-Ir L'Lo Homa, op. cit.,* p. 290.

9. For a sensitive and detailed account of Israeli efforts to develop an institutional presence in East Jerusalem, with particular emphasis on the first two and one-half years, see Gideon Weigert, *Israel's Presence in East Jerusalem,* Jerusalem: published by the author, 1973, 157 pp.

10. Duality of political status is not of potential benefit to the Arabs of Jerusalem alone. Many if not most of the Arabs now living in Israel would probably welcome the option of dual citizenship. A Palestinian political entity could provide its citizens living in Israel one level of services, such as international diplomatic protection, criminal law and education, while Israel would provide services at the local municipal level.

    For fuller discussion of the possibilities inherent in dual citizenship both for Israel's Arabs and for Jews who settle in areas that might become part of the Palestinian entity, see Saul Cohen, "Middle East Prospects for Peace, *"Jewish Frontier,* April, 1973, pp. 14-16, 19.

11. See Meron Benvenisti, *Mul HaHoma HaSegura, op. cit.,* pp. 325-327 for an eloquent plea for unity of Arabs and Jews based upon a basis of full equality.

12. For example, Allport took the position that racial attitudes are affected above

all by the degree of interracial interaction. See Gordon Allport, *The Nature of Prejudice,* Cambridge: Addison-Wesley, 1954, 537 pp.

13. Alex Weingrod and R. Mendes-Flohr, *Jewish-Arab Relationships in Jerusalem,* Jerusalem Studies Center, Institute of Urban and Regional Studies, Hebrew University of Jerusalem, March, 1976, 49 pp. This study shows that in the absence of positive steps to promote other forms of interaction, Arabs will develop separate systems which partially buffer the potentially positive impact of contact. For example, routinization of journey-to-work for Arabs employed in the Jewish sector has built into it certain protective screens, like self-contained transportation systems from point-of-origin to destination and return.

14. See Figure 1 in S. Shapiro, "Planning Jerusalem: The First Generation," 1917-1968, *Urban Geography of Jerusalem, A Companion Volume to the Atlas of Jerusalem, op. cit.,* p. 139.

15. As quoted by Zeev Vilnai in *Legends of Jerusalem, op. cit.,* p. 141 (*Isaiah.,* 60:18).

Towards
a
Solution

Resolution of the Jerusalem issue is tied to resolution of the broader Arab-Israeli conflict. Thus new political initiatives for the Holy City cannot be taken independently of a strategy that seeks solutions to the conflict. This is not to say that the Jerusalem problem cannot be addressed before there is basic agreement on a peace formula. On the contrary, unilateral steps by Israel in Jerusalem might move the more general peace process forward. To take such initiative would be to operate on the premise that the parties to the dispute should not remain inactive, relying upon time to bring forth a favorable solution. The fatalistic philosophy of letting time take its course has characterized Israeli as well as Arab strategy. It has led not to peace, but to continuation and escalation of the conflict.

PEACE OUT OF WAR

Five times in a quarter of a century, the Arab-Israeli conflict has erupted into war (1948-49, 1956, 1967, 1969-70, 1973). In the wake of each war, peace has not been directly addressed — only truces and cease fires. The Arabs have refused to do so; the Israelis have said that they can do nothing because of the Arab refusal; and external powers have limited their roles to putting a lid on Israeli military victories. Outsiders have been prepared to impose an end to fighting, not to try to impose peace. Thus the "afterword" of each war has been "this is not the time to talk peace . . . passions must die down . . . the memory of battle is too fresh . . . ."

History, however, teaches differently. The best time to talk about peace is in the wake of war, for the situation that prompts combatants to lay down their arms, never remains static. While the root cause of the Arab-Israeli conflict is Palestinian Arab rejection of Zionist settlement, there are other elements more amenable to negotiation: the attitudes of the Arab confrontation states; the interests of outside powers; the technological and territorial bases for Israel's military security. What is involved is a complex conflict system, composed of a number of agents as its subjects, and of a variety of objects. The objects constitute the environment of the system.

The agents and objects are not static; some drop out of the system of conflict as new ones enter. In 1947-48, the United Kingdom had the leverage to play a leading role in effecting peace. It chose not to do so. After 1956, Britain lost all active influence whatsoever in the Middle East dispute. In 1948-49, the United Nations, dominated by the Western world, was the central actor and might have altered the course of events. By 1973, the United Nations had become irrelevant as a force that could influence resolutions of the conflict. In 1950, the United States, Great Britain and France issued the Tripartite Declaration, pledging action to prevent any violation of frontiers or armistice lines. By 1956, the Declaration was meaningless because of the split between the United States, and France and Britain over the Suez War.

Since 1956, the United States and the U.S.S.R. have been the leading external powers in the region. But they have changed, both in their relationship to one another (from Cold War to détente) and in their relationship to other involved forces. The U.A.R. was firmly allied to the Soviet Union in 1967 and in 1970. By 1973, the Egyptians had taken a more independent stance, even though it received great quantities of Soviet weaponry just before the October War. Syria, on the other hand, was more firmly in the Soviet camp than ever before. This dependence

started with the crash program of June, 1973, whereby Soviet sur-
face-to-air missiles were supplied to it, carried through the Yom
Kippur War, and culminated with the massive shipment of Soviet
tanks in the few months following the October 1973 War that
more than replaced the 1,200 Syrian tanks that had been destroyed.

Jordan, with a significant potential to deal with Israel on
peace during the 1950s and 1960s, lost much of this potential
after 1967. The PLO emerged from obscurity to military significance after the crushing defeat suffered by the Arab confrontation states in 1967. It further gained political prestige after the
Arab oil embargo of 1973, and the Rabat declaration of 1974.
Recently, however, the Palestine guerilla movement has lost
some of its importance as a result of setbacks in the war in Lebanon during the summer of 1976. Also in these most recent years,
the Saudi Arabian role has increased; its financial strength has
provided it with considerable leverage upon the economically
hard-pressed Egyptians and the Jordanians.

Even the Maritime European role may be changing from
what has been a "hands off" policy. This is due to the threat
to Lebanese Christian survival which has provoked European
diplomatic initiatives and led to covert military support by some
European nations, as well as overt actions by Israel. The European states are also under increasing pressure by Arab OPEC-
members to take a less neutral and more overt anti-Israeli stance
in certain economic and military aspects of the conflict. Finally,
Israel's relations to the external world have changed. At its
founding the state received modest military and strong political
support from both the United States and the Soviet Union. In the
1950s, its alliance with France was the most important external
link. With the rupture of relations with France in 1967, came
ever-increasing dependence upon the United States alliance. This
has reached the point of near "client state" status since 1973.

As various actors change in importance, and as the environment of the conflict system is altered through such forces as
technological innovation and resources redistribution, conditions
responsible for bringing a halt to hostilities also change. Assumptions, therefore, that increasing delay in initiating peace negotiations will not undermine the possibilities for achieving a settlement are baseless.

The search for peace in the Arab-Israeli conflict has been continuously characterized by loss of opportunities of the moment, especially in 1967 and 1973. As a strategy for peace, the United States-imposed step-by-step disengagement plan was a missed opportunity, if not a major blunder. The conditions that prevailed in October of 1973, wherein both sides had suffered defeat as well as victory, were conditions that cried out for an all-out effort for peace. Moreover, superpower relationships, ostensibly based upon détente, could have been exploited to press the peace home.

Retrospectively, instead of battlefield negotiations at Kilometer 101 on the road to Cairo, the peace conference should have been called at Geneva directly. As it was, Geneva proved to be not a peace conference, but simply a public relations device. The conference's role was to affirm what had already been decided upon by Israel and Egypt, with the help of American interposition.[1] The excuses made at the time were based upon spurious reasoning: 1) that Israel was not prepared to discuss peace because of impending elections. (Were Japan or Germany unprepared to discuss peace because of governmental instability in 1945?); 2) that neither the United States nor Israel wanted to see the U.S.S.R. involved in peace negotiations. (Does not talking to the U.S.S.R. about peace prevent the Russians from direct involvement in what may be worse than peace, namely war?); 3) that inappropriate representation might have been achieved by the Palestinians. (Need the PLO have been the only Palestinian delegation, for could not a coalition of West and East Bankers, as well as PLO delegates have been permitted to sit with their Arab States patrons?); 4) that a European presence would have been superfluous and would have loaded the dice against Israel. (Is not much of Israel's economic fate tied to its future in Common Market Europe, and can Britain and France be kept out of the Middle Eastern armaments race by ignoring them?)

In October of 1973, those with the courage or the genuine interest in pushing for peace in the Arab-Israeli conflict should have based their strategy on the proposition that the role of external powers had reached a new height of importance within the region. The October War had brought the two super-powers closer to the brink than was acceptable to either Washington or Moscow. And Maritime Europe, because of its overwhelming concern with assuring its oil supplies, had become a new outside party to the conflict, albeit an unwilling one. Geneva could have been an historic opportunity for multi-lateral and multi-directional negotiations: Israel with outside powers, Arabs with outside powers, Israel with the Arabs, and outside powers with one another.

With regrouping of forces by both Arabs and Israelis; with the fading of memory by the superpowers of the tinderbox qualities of the situations; and with the advent of an armaments race that threatens not only to bankrupt the confrontation parties but to trigger off a new war that could bring in its wake incalculable devastation, the urgency to get on with peace initiatives is greater than ever. Time is against peace.

The External Arena of Conflict

The two geographical levels of conflict, the internal (Jews versus Arabs in former Palestine), and the external (Israel versus the Arab states) are levels that call for different strategies of negotiations and intervention. Through a combination of participation and imposition the role of outside powers in facilitating a peace between Israel and the Arab states can be as decisive now as it might have been in 1973. What the outside powers cannot do is impose a solution at the internal level of conflict. For here the issue is simple: Israel's survival and Palestinian Arab aspirations for self-determination are objectives that can only be reconciled through compromise that satisfies both peoples that they can retain for themselves the capacities to protect their own interests. Neither Jews or Arabs can be expected to leave the determination of their national fates to outside protectors.

The external arena of conflict includes the bulk of the Sinai and its adjoining waterways, the Golan Heights and, should Syria succeed in imposing its influence relatively permanently upon Lebanon, Lebanon south of the Litani. Both Arab confrontation states and Israel need something from outside powers as well as from one another. Israel, for example, needs: 1) a formal security arrangement from the United States. Such arrangement should include guarantees of arms sales and credits for a ten-year period, and the export to Israel of American scientific and technological support for military industry; 2) from Maritime Europe, admission into the European Economic Community, and 3) from the U.S.S.R., guarantees that it will not station military or advisory forces in confrontation countries, and will consider full reopening of immigration possibilities for Soviet Jewry to Israel. A demand by Israel for Soviet military and naval disengagement from bases within the Arab confrontation states would push the United States to challenge the Russians to live up to the reality as well as the public relations spirit of détente.

Israel learned many lessons for the October 1973 War, including the lesson of not taking the Arab confrontation states too lightly; of not relying upon United States political pressures; and of the positive as well as negative attributes of extending its military lines deep into the administered territories. It learned that the impact of a massive initial Arab attack is too devastating to be acceptable, and that it can be averted only by a first-strike military strategy; that military doctrine calls for greater reliance upon mobile forces and avoidance of undermanned fixed bases; that deliberately established agricultural forward point settlements may serve as strategic "trip-wires," but need to be armed with modern, heavy weapons if they are not to become tactical liabilities; and that over-dependence upon outside military suppliers and relaxation of efforts to improve indigenous arms superiority can lead to diplomatic blackmail and military catastrophe. Israel's possession of the territories did not ward off attack, but it did provide time and security for the successful counter-attack.

When territorial compromises are made by Israel, they are likely to become a basis for negotiation with the outside powers, as well as with the Arabs. This has already been the case in the Sinai and Golan disengagement agreements, although omission of the Soviet Union in the bargaining may yet prove to have been a major liability in the struggle for peace. Arab confrontation states are less in need of guarantees. What the Arabs require is return of territory. Other Arab objectives, such as access to military equipment and modern technology, can, of course, be spelled out in formal treaty arrangements. But oil revenues, and the general leverage of oil resources are worth more to the Arabs than treaty guarantees from either the West or from the U.S.S.R. Hard currency can purchase all the needed hardware and support systems from a number of competing national vendors.

With respect to Israeli-Arab confrontation state relations, it is obvious that neither of the old formulas — first peace and then territorial withdrawal (Israeli), or first territorial withdrawal and then peace (Arab) — are now tenable. The focus must be on the *process of interaction,* rather than on the diplomatic formalities.

The charge has been made both outside and inside Israel that a major cause of the October war was the failure of the Israeli government to display its proposed territorial map in unambiguous terms. It is easy to draw maps and counter-maps. Had there been some assurance that peace would flow from territorial compromise, maps surely would have been presented by Israel at the first opportunity. But given the unrelenting Arab attitude towards Israel, Soviet intervention on behalf of the Arabs, French alignment with the Arab cause, and the hostile Third World climate, Israel could hardly have been expected to separate the territorial issue from an overall peace settlement. Similarly, from the standpoint of the Arab confrontation states, peace agreements cannot be tied solely to Israeli withdrawal from territories. Specific steps that would lead to a resolution of the Arab refugee problem and assurance of a West Bank Arab political entity are also requirements.

What are some of the processes that might be put forward to link *territories* and *peace?* One has to do with demilitarization, carried out by joint military surveillance teams. Israel's price for future disengagements in the Sinai is likely to be guaranteed freedom of navigation for its vessels in the Suez Canal, the Gulf of Aqaba and the Red Sea (See Figure 15). Israel would also seek assurance that would prevent the Sinai from becoming an Egyptian military staging base, and Gaza from falling under Egyptian military control. Until now, the Israeli withdrawal from the Sinai has been accompanied by separation of forces by the military inadequate and (from an Israeli standpoint) politically unreliable United Nations forces, and by an American "third party" surveillance effort. Dependence on such external guarantees has its limitations.

From the record of the past it seems clear that United Nations forces are less desirable and reliable as guarantors than those of great powers who take part in the peace negotiations. But as supplements, if not alternatives to intervening outside forces, joint Egyptian-Israeli military surveillance teams offer considerable advantages. If Israelis and Egyptians could directly negotiate a cease-fire on the western side of the Suez Canal, they should be able to develop surveillance arrangements. For example, navigation of international waters could be assured by a small fleet of Israeli, Egyptian and neutral war craft, operating in the northern and southern approaches to the Canal through the Gulf of Suez, the Straits of Tiran, the Red Sea and the Straits of

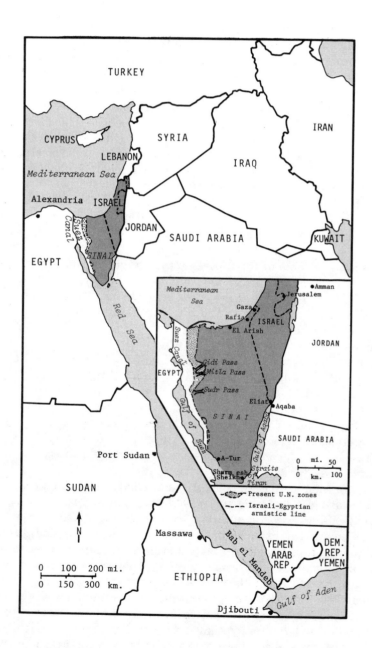

Fig. 15. The Middle East as Arena for Peace-Keeping

Bab el Mandeb. Sharm esh Sheikh could serve as the naval base for the fleet or the Israeli base could remain at Ophira and the Egyptians could develop a new one on the Gulf of Suez. Under such circumstances, the territorial disposition of the "rock" could be more easily negotiated, perhaps as a bi-national or international base; so could a land corridor from Eilat to Sharm. Cyprus and Massawa, Djibouti or even the Seychelles could serve as back-up bases for this fleet. Similarly, lightly-armed Israeli and Egyptian gendarmes could jointly man the listening posts on the Sinai pass reaches, while more heavily-armored forces of the two states might together patrol the Sinai coast. In the event that an American surveillance team should be required at Sharm esh Sheikh, as in the Sinai, it could be based on the Island of Tiran.

The same kinds of joint military arrangements could be made along a new cease fire line in the Golan Heights with both Israeli and Syrian troops. Should Lebanon survive as an independent country, similar Lebanese-Israeli patrols could be organized in the area south of the Litani River.

But interaction processes cannot be limited to the military sphere. Certain economic issues have clear security implications. In connection with the second Sinai disengagement (the Egyptian-Israeli Accord on the Sinai, September 1, 1975), one form of American interposition was a guaranteed supply of petroleum to Israel, as the quid pro quo for Israeli return of the Abu Rudeis oil fields to Egypt. Israel is now developing offshore fields in the Gulf of Suez at A-Tur and offshore at Sharm esh Sheikh. Compensation for withdrawal by Israel from these Sinai oil areas could take the form of a contract agreement with Egypt for a joint production and marketing company in which Israel would have a minority share. Such a company's major operating but non-owning partner could be a Western corporation so that Egypt would not have to participate directly. Its economic interests would be protected by its ownership status.

Still another example of economic interaction in a sector that has security implications is nuclear power. Israel and Egypt are in the process of planning nuclear energy reactors with American assistance. Both nations fear that the other may take advantage of the technology to further the development of nuclear weapons. A plan for interaction might be to build *both* Israeli and Egyptian reactors in a new kind of nuclear park — an artificial island built off the Sinai coast. Siting nuclear plants off-shore has considerable advantage from the standpoint of minimizing risk from nuclear accidents and for dissipating cooling waters. Moreover, the possibility that both sides might share their technological experiences in interactive fashion directly or through on-the-spot American supervision, makes such a bold initiative even more attractive.

Geneva

Jewish settlement in North Sinai and on the western half of the Golan Heights is likely to be accelerated, especially as a concommitant to territorial compromises elsewhere. In addition to agricultural and urban settlements in these areas (with their primary "trip-wire" functions), the need for stationing mobile military forces there probably makes mandatory the continued status of North Sinai and part of the Golan as Israeli-administered territories. Eventually, however, these two regions should be able to acquire unique demilitarized characteristics that would carry them to new and different political stages. The Golan Heights could be opened to the return of Druze who lived on the Golan before the 1967 war. The Heights could also be opened to settlement by Druze presently living in the Galilee. Such a mixed Israeli-Druze region might be accorded *special regional autonomy status* within Israel, as a means of encouraging Druze self-fulfillment. Alternatively, the Golan could be set aside as an Israeli-Syrian condominium, with focus on Druze autonomy and development in the region, but allowing for continued Jewish and Muslim settlement.

In North Sinai, major Israeli efforts to develop a "Riviera" from north east of Rafia to a few kilometers of El Arish, might create a very large and unique tourist area for the crowded, urbanized Israeli population, and for overseas recreation home owners and short-term visitors. While Rafia Approaches would be linked territorially to Israel, the major portion of North Sinai (from El Arish to An Nachal and east to the Gulf of Aqaba shore) might eventually become part of the Palestinian West Bank entity, either as a fourth region, or as part of the Gaza district. Whatever the case, to protect both the approaches to Israel's southern coastal plain and Eilat, North Sinai would have to have special status as a permanent Israeli military base. In the same way, Egypt would expect to have a permanent military base on the east bank of the Suez Canal.

The Internal Arena of Conflict

The internal arena of conflict is the West Bank, Gaza, Jerusalem and, when it serves as "Fatahland", Southern Lebanon. In this arena, the role of outside powers and the Arab confrontation states can be of limited utility in imposing and guaranteeing a peace. For the very survival of Israel and the Palestinian Arabs is at stake, and people do not negotiate away their existence. Ironically for Jordan, the more it shifts its role to that of a confrontation state, the less it may be able to involve itself as a principal in the negotiations.

An underlying assumption in the quest for peace in the internal arena is that a Palestinian entity will emerge, either west of Jordan or as part of a unified Arab state straddling both sides of the Jordan. Israel's refusal to take the initiative on the subject of a Palestinian state has weakened the underpinnings of its peace initiatives. The Palestinian Arabs are a fact in every sense of the word, including the geopolitical.

It took the emergence of the Palestinian Liberation Organization as a significant element on the international scene to stir the Israelis. It would be another missed opportunity if military reverses suffered by the PLO in the war in Lebanon were to be used by Israeli policy-makers as a rationalization to try once again to shelve the issue of the Palestinians until negotiations with the Arab confrontation states were successfully concluded.

One immediate step that could be taken by Israel, independent of full-scale negotiations on the resolution of the West Bank's future, would be to establish autonomous Arab political districts in the West Bank: in Judea centered around Hebron, in Samaria around Nablus, and in Gaza. Israel could hope that these regions would affiliate with Jordan in a loose federation (there could be two national capitals, a summer one at Amman and a winter one at Jericho). However, it is more likely that the Palestinians would find a way to organize themselves independent of the Jordanian government. What the Palestinians do with the political future of the West Bank should be left to the Palestinians. Israel can let matters take their course by withdrawing the current military government's responsibility for civilian affairs. Israel can take the role of a power occupying another state, with military withdrawal dependent upon the timing and terms of the latter's suit for peace. Proposals to permit an autonomous Arab regime in the West Bank have been sporadically considered within Israeli governmental circles, especially after 1967 and 1973. They have not, however, centered on the concept that grass-roots achieved Arab independence would have far greater incentive to come to peace terms with an occupying power.

In effect, Israel can say to the Palestinian Arabs in the West Bank: "We have left a rudimentary administrative structure based on three regions — you take it from here."[2] The Arabs would have to fill the political vacuum through their own devices, Israeli military preventing the return of Jordanian troops or of Palestine Liberation Organization paramilitary forces, but otherwise not interfering in the development of a new West Bank political system. It is to be expected that the struggle for political control would be sharp among the four leadership groups: new and traditional West Bank factions, the Jordanian monarchy and the PLO.

Israel would continue to use its military forces: to quash internal Arab political terror, to assure Jewish settlement in border sections of the West Bank, and to guarantee freedom of access for Jews to the West Bank, and Arabs to Israel. Its forces would also continue to guard the Jordan River security line.

A major focus for West Bank Jewish settlement, which until now has been essentially agricultural (Kiryat Arba just north of Hebron is an exception), should be large urban centers or "hinges". Such hinges, unlike Kiryat Arba, ought to adjoin or be relatively close to Israeli territory. These hinges are likely to be more effective "trip wires" than agricultural settlements, and more important as deterrents to the resumption of full-scale hostilities between Israel and outside states. The peaceful relationship between the ports of Eilat and Aqaba is a case in point. The proposed port city of Yamit in the Rafia Approaches is an example of a well located and well conceived urban hinge.

Israel can take the initiative, formalizing the political and military implications of the Allon Plan and some of the Dayan versions thereof.[3] Israel can afford to give the Arabs responsibility for finding a way to organize a West Bank political system, for it has the military power to safeguard itself against the use of the West Bank as a base of significant military operations against the Jewish state. In the first stage, the Israeli military presence doubtlessly would maintain its present posture within urbanized areas. Gradually, these forces could be confined to the countryside and replaced by an Arab gendarmerie in the urban areas subject to the emerging legitimate government or governments. Israel can make it clear to the West Bank residents that their political destiny is their responsibility. It can encourage the process whereby forging of this destiny will not have to await a peace, but can precede and be a first stage in this peace.

The processes of immigration, both Jewish and Arab, can also become a lever for peace, rather than a consequence of the peace. Israel's lifting of controls over civilian affairs in the West Bank would have to include giving West Bank Arab authorities unlimited rights to regulate the return of former residents and immigration in general. Granted that the return of potential terrorists could create a threat for Israel, the presence of Israeli military forces in Judea, Samaria and Gaza surely can keep the problem in bounds. Indeed, the ability of Israelis to keep hostile Palestinians in check from bases in lightly populated parts of the West Bank is greater than their ability to keep them in check while they operate from Lebanon, Syria or Jordan. A West Bank militarily dominated by Israel would be a trap for Arab terrorists should the PLO try to shift its base of operations there for terrorist campaigns against Israel.

The question of the return of additional Palestinians to Israel, as distinct from their return to the West Bank, can be tied to developments in the West Bank. Peaceful behavior towards Israel by the Palestinian population of the West Bank, operating under its own civilian controls, would be a precondition to any Israeli decision to permit additional Arab residence in Israel. Such behavior would include guarantee of freedom of movement to Israelis and limited settlement possibilities for Israelis in the Palestinian state. Moreover, Israel's attitude towards enlarging the permanent Arab population of Israel through immigration could be linked to the offsetting Jewish immigration factor — Soviet Jewry.

If numbers of Jewish emigrants were allowed by the U.S.S.R. to increase dramatically (possibly to double or triple the annual number of 36,400 in 1972, and 33,451 in 1973), Israel would feel far more secure in allowing a significant number of Arabs to return as citizens of Israel. For example, the inflow of 300,000 Soviet Jews in a five year period could make it politically and defensively possible for Israel to absorb 100,000 Arabs who might wish to resettle at or near areas formerly inhabited by them. The return of Palestinian Arabs would be a subject of negotiation, not between Israel and such Arab states as Syria, Lebanon, Egypt or Jordan, but rather between Israel, the West Bank governmental structure, and the individual Arab. In some cases the immigration could be two-step; first from Arab countries to the West Bank, and second, on an individual basis, to Israel, possibly after trial periods with daily work permits in Israel from West Bank residential points. Jerusalem should prove a particularly valuable "staging base" for returning Palestinians. Its urbanized setting, its employment base and its Jewish majority provide some concept to would-be returnees of what the ambience of Jaffa and Haifa might hold out as a place of permanent residence.

Finally, the possibilities for long-term accommodation between Israel and the Arabs relate to very specific forms of economic, social and political integration. Social and economic interaction has been promoted by the "open borders" policy along the Jordan and in a small way with the "good fence" policy along the Lebanese border. Even broader forms of interaction have been encouraged by Israel's granting West Bank inhabitants access to work opportunities in Israel. Israel can seize the initiative to press forward with another form of integration - a form of dual citizenship opportunities for those who desire. Arabs living in Israel would be allowed West Bank citizenship along with their Israeli citizenship, and Jews settling in the West Bank could request West Bank citizenship from local Arab political authorities to go along with their Israeli status.

While there are very few Jews living in the territories, if any, who would request dual citizenship, some of Israel's Arab citizens might do so. An Israeli Arab holding Palestinian citizenship could look to the latter to provide for international status and to fulfill certain national rights and responsibilities (e.g., higher education, national gendarmerie, elections to national parliament). Israeli civic rights and responsibilities could be discharged at the local governmental level. The same could apply to Jews living in Israeli settlements in the West Bank who would be obliged to discharge local municipal responsibilities under national West Bank codes, whether or not they opted for dual citizenship.

Just as Jews in the territories would probably wish Israeli citizenship only (with permanent West Bank residence rights), so many Arabs now living in Israel who prefer to adopt Palestinian citizenship might wish to give up Israeli citizenship in exchange for permanent Israeli residence rights. The only practical distinction between Israeli citizenship and permanent resident status for Arabs would be change in passport and higher educational rights, and possibly in social security and trade union benefits, for even now Israeli Arab citizens are not required to serve in the Israeli armed forces.

A New Threat to Maintaining a Heterogeneous City

The problem of nurturing the Arab presence is encountering major new obstacles triggered by Arab war strategy and terror tactics. These may boomerang to endanger the position of Jerusalem's Arabs. If the Arab-Israeli conflict should be renewed, there is the strong possibility that war will once again be brought to the gates of Jerusalem. Jordan's decision to coordinate military and other policies with Syria through a Syrian-Jordanian Supreme Command Council involves preparations for establishing an active third front in the conflict. Moreover, Saudi Arabian-Jordanian cooperation could lead to a fourth front at the Gulf of Aqaba. The Palestinians of the West Bank might then be induced to join the fray through sabotage efforts and perhaps even through appearing as PLO units via these eastern fronts.

Even if the Palestinians should confine themselves to local acts of terrorism and sabotage, Jordan's shift in policy to becoming a confrontation party poses a military threat to Israel. Special security precautions have to be taken in the West Bank and especially in Jerusalem. Israeli military and civil defense authorities are already contemplating the possibility that the city will become an active part of the front, as it was in 1948 and 1967. As difficult as conflict may be for Jerusalem's Jews, it could have nightmarish consequences for Jerusalem's Arabs, for the Jewish state at war could not tolerate a fifth column within its gates in Jerusalem. Constituting only 27% of the city's population, and now surrounded by large-scale Jewish housing areas, the Arab residents can have no illusions. Flight or massed evacuations of Arabs occurred as part of the process of war in 1948 in Jaffa, in Haifa, in Lod, in Ramleh, in Safed, and could occur again in Jerusalem.

Thus, King Hussein of Jordan is playing with fire in entering confrontation politics so that he can "get a piece of the negotiations." The same is the case for those Jerusalem Arabs who are in league with terrorists or condone terror tactics. If conflict should erupt on the eastern front, compounded by an increase in local acts of sabotage, the Palestinians are not likely to be able to sit the war out as they did in 1973. And as a consequence of such a war, the Arab presence could be eliminated from Jerusalem.

The purpose of the above is not to indulge in idle speculation, sketching out an improbable scenario. It is, rather, to call attention to a real and pressing danger. Perhaps American policymakers or World Christian interests see the new Jordanian stance as part of the war of nerves, the ultimate objective of which is to pressure Israel into negotiating with the Arabs to assure a return to something like the pre-1967 borders. American decisions to provide massive shipments of arms to Jordan may be viewed in this connection. Perhaps, too, King Hussein feels that confrontation politics will lead to concessions by Israel on Jerusalem that will return a Jordanian presence to the city. But it is much more likely that threats to the unity and integrity of Jerusalem, if combined with conflict, could lead to a radical resolution of the Jerusalem problem — the emergence of an all-Jewish city through removal of the Arab populace. Such an eventuality would not only be a catastrophe for the Arabs, it would mark a disastrous turn of events for Jews in their search for peace and accommodation with the Arabs.

BANKRUPTCY OF INTERNATIONALIZATION AS A SOLUTION

The geopolitical struggle for Jerusalem today is a struggle of competing nationalisms. For Israeli nationalism, Jerusalem is a territorial imperative. For Palestinian Arab nationalism, loss of control of East Jerusalem means an indefensible West Bank in the absence of political conditions which remove the need for Arab concern over security. In such a struggle, whatever compromise is effected cannot be made without diminishing the political sovereignty of one of the entities. This at least is one of the two arguments for internationalization of Jerusalem — the "no win, no loss" argument. The second argument is viewed by its proponents as a moral imperative: that Jerusalem belongs to more than Israeli Jews and Palestinian Arabs; rather, that the city is holy to three great faiths, Christian, Muslim and Jewish, and that guardianship of Jerusalem should be entrusted to a neutral international body.

Internationalization as a Christian Religious Position

The Christian attitude towards political internationalization of Jerusalem was shaped by events that began with the introduction into Palestine of the capitulations system in the seventeenth century, first to France and then to Russia. In the mid-eighteenth century a Turkish Imperial decree established the Regime of the Status Quo, whereby Christian sects were given ownership and control of their Holy Sites. This decree later was extended to include Muslim and Jewish Holy Places.

In the past century the Christian presence in Jerusalem increased dramatically as a result of the 1840 enactment by Turkey of reforms and privileges. The Consular Corps in Jerusalem acquired wide jurisdiction and protective power, promoting the development of missionary and philanthropic work, church building and pilgrimages. Weakened by Mohammed Ali's rebellion (1839), dependent upon the Western powers during the Crimean War (1853-1860), and powerless in the Crisis in Lebanon (1860), Turkey's ability to steer an independent course in Palestine was undermined. The end became clear when the Young Turks failed to find a political solution to the Empire's problems. Eventually the West entered the Holy Land directly with the British military occupation. Subsequent Mandatory rule reshaped Jerusalem's administrative and physical structure, adding a "new" city to the "old". From the very outset of the Mandate, Britain was seen by other European states as representing the Christian powers. The entry of British troops into Jerusalem on December of 1917, was regarded by many as the return of the city to Christian control — 700 years after the fall of the last Crusader Kingdom.[4]

Attempts to introduce an international dimension with respect to Jerusalem were part of the diplomatic events that led up to the Mandate and shaped its terms. The Sykes-Picot Agreement of 1916 called for an international administration for much of the land west of the Jordan, the area from Jerusalem to Jaffa to Gaza. More directly, the Mandatory terms included reference to an international structure in Jerusalem at the insistence of the Vatican, France, Spain and other European countries. In Article 14 of the Mandate, there was provision for a special International Commission to study and define rights and claims in connection with the Holy Places.[5] Even though such a Commission was not established, the British never formally rejected the notion that the Catholic powers did not have a special role to play in Jerusalem. Throughout the Mandatory Period, Great Britain insisted that it was acting on behalf of the European-controlled League of Nations in governing as a sacred trust the Old City with its religious shrines and settlements. While the language of internationalization nearly always made reference to all three faiths, emphasis in practice was on Christian concerns.

Internationalization of Jerusalem became a key element of various British proposals for the partition or cantonization of Palestine (See Figure 16).[6] In 1933, a partition plan proposed an international administration for Jerusalem and Bethlehem. In 1935-36, cantonization plans called for a special entity for Jerusalem with an economic hinterland that included surrounding agricultural settlements and even the Dead Sea's minerals. The Peel Commission in 1937, and the Woodhead Commission in 1938, put forward the same general notion, and the League of Nations in 1941 called for Jerusalem to be a Special Federal Territory.

Other proposals that included an international status for Jerusalem were The Morrison-Grady Plan of 1946, and the Jewish Agency's Partition plans of 1947. These were all preludes to the Report of the United Nations Special Commission on Palestine (UNSCOP) in 1947, which called for an international regime in Greater Jerusalem as part of the Partition Plan. Loss of dominant status by the Western and Christian powers in the United Nations; the bankruptcy of the United Nations Partition Plan; the decline in numbers and influence of the Christian population of Jerusalem since 1948; and the rising salience of Jewish and Arab interests have not eliminated the Christian interest and stake in internationalization. But recent events have shunted aside this political mechanism as a realistic solution.[7] One might argue that plans for internationalization have become a code word for a kind of Christian pseudo-colonialism, at a time when the focus in Jerusalem has shifted to its being mainly the arena for Jewish-Arab relations.

Internationalization from Israeli and Arab Geopolitical Standpoints

There has been no single Jewish/Israeli position on the geopolitical status of Jerusalem, just as there has been no single

Arab/Palestinian position. Moreover, positions taken by various bodies with delegated authority to represent the two peoples often have been equivocal. The situation is further complicated today in that one formal body, the Israeli government, represents the Jewish side, while the Arabs lack a voice to represent their interests with similarly vested sovereign authority.

With these as caveats against oversimplifications, it is nevertheless possible to offer some generalizations. Jews accepted internationalization as part of the partition package — the price for Jewish statehood. As Halpern puts it: "There was hardly an aspect of the U.N. Partition Plan which was so repugnant to the Jews as the internationalization of Jerusalem."[8] Internationalization was accepted as the price for partition and on the assumption that after ten years a Jewish majority in the city would vote to join Israel. Israeli acceptance held through much of the first phase of the Arab-Israeli War of Independence. From then on the concept of internationalization rapidly lost credence among the Israelis. A major consequence of the bankruptcy of the United Nations Partition Plan was that Israel, emerging victoriously from the war, declared internationalization plans for the city to be null and void.

The Arabs vehemently opposed Jerusalem's internationalization at the time that Jews were willing to accept it, just as they opposed the entire Partition Plan. After their military defeats in 1948-49, the Arab League States reversed themselves by announcing their support of internationalization. King 'Abdallah, on the other hand, was quite content with the status quo that had left the Old City and East Jerusalem in Jordanian lands. He, like the Israelis, now preferred partition of the city to internationalization.

The UNSCOP plan of 1947 offered the specific proposal to organize Arab and Jewish states, linked with internationalized Jerusalem, in an economic union. The internationalized zone would join Bethlehem to Jerusalem, and include the suburbs of both cities. It would have been administered by a special international regime in a relationship with the United Nations' Trusteeship Council. Described as the City of Jerusalem, the internationalized zone was proposed as a *corpus separatum,* extending from Motza on the west, to Shuafat on the north, to Abu Dis on the east, to south of Bethlehem. The area was considerably more extensive in the east and south than is united Jerusalem

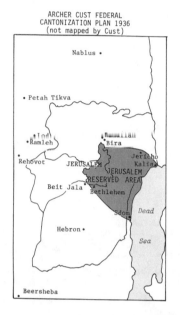

Fig. 16. Past Proposals for Internationalization of Jerusalem

JEWISH AGENCY PLAN 1946

MORRISON & GRADY 1946

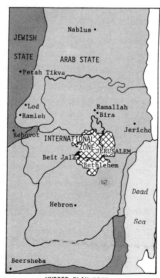

UNSCOP PLAN 1947

today, although not as extensive as what is now the Jerusalem metropolitan area. The *corpus separatum* would hold 100,000 Jews and 100,000 Arabs (note the similarity in proportions to what now holds for Metropolitan Jerusalem), and residents could opt for citizenship in either the Jewish or the Arab states (See Figure 16).[9]

THE BASIS FOR JEWISH ATTITUDES

The Jewish attitude on Jerusalem's status was initially based upon the hope than an internationalized and demilitarized city would spare it from the ravages of war. But the battle for Jerusalem, characterized by the seige and efforts to lift it, dashed these hopes. The reshaping of this attitude was due not merely to the objective realities of Arab military intervention in Jerusalem, and failure of the United Nations to develop mechanisms that would assure Jews of their security. It was also due to political pressure from Jewish Jerusalemites upon the Israeli government — the consequence of the wartime events.

Throughout the battle for Jerusalem, Jerusalem's Jews registered their bitterness at the Tel Aviv government for having been left in isolation to face the Arab Legion, starvation, and thirst. Dov Joseph understated these feelings when, describing conditions after the end of the first truce, he wrote, "There was a feeling abroad in Jerusalem that not all that could have been done for the capital had been done."[10] Dissatisfaction with decisions on complex issues had provoked resentment in Jerusalem: the quantity of arms and munitions to be allotted to the Jerusalem front by the Hagana High Command; the quality of training of the forces assigned to Jerusalem; the slower pace of manpower mobilization elsewhere in the country; the amount of food and drugs mustered for convoys trying to break the siege — these all placed great strain on the relations between Jerusalemites and the central government. This was coupled with the grim truth that Jerusalemites, penned up in physical, political and psychological isolation behind their siege walls, *had* suffered more than the rest of the country.

While most of Jerusalem's travails were overcome with the conclusion of the first cease-fire, bitterness remained as a result of the events that took place during the second round of battle (July 9-19, 1948). Overall strategic objectives of the Israeli High Command during the second outbreak of fighting, while understandable from a military standpoint, nevertheless increased Jerusalemites' level of concern and frustration. Clearing the Jerusalem Corridor received priority over the two military objectives paramount to those inside Jerusalem: reopening the road to Mount Scopus via Sheikh Jarrah, and recapturing the Old City. Success of the priority objective secured Jerusalem, but failure of the other two left the Arab Legion as an unwelcome neighbor inside of Jerusalem. Moreover, as late as September 6, well into the second truce of July 19 - October 14, *Davar Yerushalayim*[11] voiced the complaint that "there is still discrimination against Jerusalem." Reference was to the prevailing food situation. Jerusalem continued to suffer from lack of fresh milk and meat, while other parts of the country experienced relatively few shortages. This followed the bitterness experienced during the first truce (June 11 - July 9) over the action of the United Nations Truce Commission. There had been constant tussles between the Jewish authorities in Jerusalem and the Commission over how much food and clothing would be allowed by the United Nations to get through to Jerusalem. Indeed, convoys did not arrive regularly until the third week of the truce.[12]

Resentment against the United Nations was exacerbated by the nagging suspicion that the Tel Aviv government was still not fully committed to putting Jerusalem first; indeed, there was some question as to its commitment to a sovereign Jewish future for West Jerusalem. This suspicion was heightened when, on July 7, two days before the end of the first truce, Foreign Minister Shertok (Sharett) wrote to Dov Joseph, (then representative of the Provisional Government to the U.N. Mediator, and head of the Jerusalem Emergency Committee), that the Israeli Cabinet did not consider that continuation of the truce should be conditional upon renewal of the water supply to Jerusalem.[13] Reference was to provisions of the truce calling for reopening the water pipeline from Ras al Ayn to Jerusalem. The Arabs who controlled the pumping stations at Ras al Ayn and Latrun refused to restart the pumps and the Truce Commission took no steps to try to force compliance.

On August 2, 1948, the Israeli provisional government declared Jerusalem as Israeli-occupied territory under a military governorship, but a minority of the cabinet was still willing to accept internationalization as a compromise.[14] Jerusalem's pressures on the Israeli central authority culminated in a formal demand on September 26, 1948, by the Jerusalem delegation who were members of the Provisional Government that Jerusalem be incorporated into Israel.[15] By this time, Tel Aviv was receptive and three days later the government decided to insist on inclusion of West Jerusalem within Israel at all costs. The Corridor had been fully secured through Israeli victories in the second round of fighting that had gained control of the railroad, Lydda Airport and most of the water pipeline route. The entrance to the corridor in Emeq Ayyalon had been so widened that it was now the Jordanians who were surrounded at Latrun. The western edges of Jerusalem had also been extended and widened at Ein Kerem, Malha and Mount Herzl.

Moreover, the actions of the United Nations Mediator, Count Bernadotte, had undermined any residual support for internationalization that might have remained within the Provisional Government. On June 27, the Mediator announced a plan that would give 'Abdallah all of the Arab areas of Palestine, plus the city of Jerusalem. In his "Suggestions for the Future of Palestine," he called for inclusion of the city as part of an Arab state, with municipal autonomy for the Jewish community. Special arrangements for the protection of the Holy Places were to be provided. The city would be demilitarized and controlled by 6,000 United Nations armed troops.[16]

When fighting was renewed shortly thereafter, the Mediator called for demilitarization of the city as a whole. He changed his plan in what proved to be his last report to the United Nations, which arrived the day after his assassination on September 17, by members of the Jewish Stern terrorist group, LEHI (Fighters for Freedom of Israel). The report recommended that Jerusalem be internationalized and placed under effective United Nations control, with maximum feasible autonomy for the Arab and Jewish communities, and safeguards for access to the Holy Places.

The damage that the Mediator did to undermine a support base for internationalization within the Jewish community was considerable, but so were Arab actions during the truce periods. In August, during the second truce, the Latrun pumping station, now in no-man's land and under United Nations protection, was blown up by Arab irregulars. Moreover, the main road to Jeru-

salem, part of which was held by the Arabs, was not allowed to be
passed by United Nations' supervised convoys until October 15,
despite truce provisions. As a result, Jerusalem had to depend on
the "Burma Road", and upon a temporary pipeline opened on
August 12 from Hulda, paralleling this road (See Figure 5). The
road ran from just east of Hulda, via Beit Jis, Beit Susin and Beit
Mahzir to Saris on the main Jerusalem road. The route skirted
Latrun and Shaar HaGay. Opened on May 18, with the use of
mules over a three-mile stretch, it became operational for motor-
ized vehicles along its entire length on June 11. Later, the Road of
Valor (Heroes' Road) supplanted the Burma Road. This second
road, opened on December 13, was more removed from the Arab-
held Latrun salient, running one to two kilometers south of the
western half of the Burma Road, extending from Hulda to Har-
tuv. From there, the route followed an existing road north to
Shaar HaGay, picking up the main highway to Jerusalem at that
point. During the truce, and portent of things to come, the Arabs
denied Jews promised access to the Holy Places in the Old City
and the Mount of Olives cemetery.

On February 21, 1949, the Israeli Provisional Government announced that Western Jerusalem was no longer to be considered
occupied territory and abolished military government. Israel continued to favor internationalization of the Old City until the
spring of 1949. Then it shifted to a policy of functional internationalization of the Holy Places only — a policy which it holds
to this day. The United Nations would not agree to such limitations of its authority. Instead, on December 10, 1949, the General
Assembly reissued a called-for international control over the entire city and its environs through the Trusteeship Council.[17] Israel's immediate response was an announcement in the Knesset
by Ben Gurion, reaffirming a statement made to that body on
December 5, that Jerusalem was an integral part of Israel,
not to be forcefully torn apart from the rest of the country.[18] This
announcement was followed by a decision to have the Knesset
relocate permanently to Jerusalem, the Provisional Parliament
meeting there on December 26, 1949. On January 23, 1950, the
Knesset moved that Jerusalem had always been the capital of
Israel. The final important Israeli diplomatic action in Jerusalem
was to transfer the Foreign Ministry to the capital on July 12,
1953.

Had the Arabs accepted partition rather than war, and had

either economic union or a federated state subsequently emerged, then a special status for Jerusalem would have been politically and operationally feasible. This could have been accomplished either under an international regime or as a federal capital with an international body to supervise the Holy Places. Since 1948-49, and with each of the subsequent four wars, changes have come in the Israeli national territorial consciousness, with specific territories acquiring new values and sentiments. Today, a unified Jewish Jerusalem has become intrinsic to the Israeli perception of viability and territorial integrity. It is difficult to conceive of Israel's agreeing to a new repartition of Jerusalem under any circumstances except military defeat in a new war. A united Jerusalem is as strong a geopolitical imperative to Israel as was Biafra to Nigeria, the Katanga to Zaire, Irian to Indonesia, the Baltic States, East Prussia and Eastern Poland to the Soviet Union, Tibet to the People's Republic of China, Kurdistan to Iraq, and the South to Sudan.

THE BASIS FOR ARAB ATTITUDES

The Jews alone did not doom the United Nations plans to internationalize Jerusalem. The Arabs, too, subverted these plans: first, by their attempts to seize the entire city; then, by the negative Jordanian position in the United Nations; and finally, by Jordanian diplomatic actions in annexing Eastern Jerusalem.

King 'Abdallah first made it clear that he had rejected the concept of Jerusalem's internationalization when, during the first armistice period, he sought to persuade Egypt and Iraq to join the Arab Legion in an all-out attack to take all of Jerusalem.[19] After the final armistice agreements, other Arab governments came around to endorsing internationalization of the city as whole, but 'Abdallah, by then in control of East Jerusalem, strongly opposed the stand. He proclaimed himself firmly in defense of the Arab character of the Holy City and opposing internationalization.[20]

'Abdallah's attitudes on Jerusalem were tied to his views of the West Bank as a whole. The area occupied by the Arab Legion was annexed de facto on March 17, 1949. In the following October, a National Arab Council was established in Gaza with the former Mufti of Jerusalem, Hajj Amin al Husseini, as President. 'Abdallah reacted by declaring the West Bank part of the Arab

Hashemite Kingdom on December, 1950. De jure action followed on April 24, 1950, with annexation of the West Bank confirmed by the Jordanian Parliament.[21]

'Abdallah had a very special feeling about Jerusalem, but made no move to transfer his political base there. Certainly, the strength within the city of the ex-Mufti, his mortal enemy, and the widespread sentiments of Arab Jerusalemites in favor of Palestinian separatism were factors in his decision. Ultimately, 'Abdallah was to die in Jerusalem, assassinated by the ex-Mufti's followers in al-Aqsa Mosque on June 28, 1951.

Under King Hussein, Jordan continued its teasing romance with Jerusalem, promising much and delivering little. On August 6, 1953, the Jordanian Parliament proclaimed Jerusalem the alternate capital of the Hashemite Kingdom, resolving to meet there periodically. In fact, Parliament met in Jerusalem only once, and the cabinet twice during the period of Jordan occupancy. In November of 1954, Hussein announced that he would build a summer palace in the Holy City. But the foundations at Tel al-Ful, site of King Saul's Israelite capital, were not laid for another decade. At the outbreak of the Six Day War, the palace was still unfinished. Again, when Israel's new Knesset building was opened in July, 1966, Jordan's reaction was to declare Jerusalem its "spiritual capital." The practical meaning of this was a call to Arab organizations to hold conventions and meetings there.

Israel's initiatives to strengthen its presence in Jerusalem, thereby undermining internationalization, were followed by Jordanian responses to assert the Jordanian presence. The difference was that Israel physically established its capital in Jerusalem; the Jordanians' political priority was, in reality, Amman.

CHANGING GEOPOLITICAL CONTEXT OF JERUSALEM'S POLITICAL STATUS

From an Israeli point of view, internationalization has become even more of an anachronism now that the city has been reunified. For Jordan and the Palestinians, the reaction to internationalization is now more ambiguous. The Jordanian position is for a return to the situation in 1946, with Jews being allowed to live in East Jerusalem and Arabs in West Jerusalem. Even though dual citizenship would be a possibility, the Jordanian stance would inevitably lead to renewed partition of the city because ultimate agreement on Jerusalem will most probably depend upon Arab control of the West Bank. Because of Israel's opposition to repartition of Jerusalem, the current Jordanian position may not be fixed. Moreover, Saudi Arabian pressures for internationalization may also bring about a change in the Jordanian position. If internationalization is "half a loaf," then it may be better than none, at least for King Hussein. In 1961, Hussein put it this way: "Jerusalem is no longer a Jordanian problem but a Moslem problem, an Arab and a Christian problem . . . . we cannot give up our rights to Jerusalem, for they go back more than a thousand years."[22] The Jordanian capacity to aspire to regaining the role of Master and Guardian of the Old City has been further eroded by appointment of the PLO as sole representative of the Palestinian people at the 1974 Rabat Arab summit meeting.

The PLO can be expected to reject the old Arab States line favoring internationalization of Jerusalem, because the PLO rejects the very concept of partition.[23] Moreover, many of those living on the West Bank, including East Jerusalemites, express sentiment for the status quo ante, which would involve at least some form of Arab control of East Jerusalem, rather than internationalization. If King Hussein were given an opportunity to return to the negotiating table as a central actor, he would probably hold out for an Arab East Jerusalem, rather than internationalization.

In summarizing the Jewish and Arab case against internationalization, it is instructive to refer to the words of Ben Gurion and 'Abdallah at that moment in history when Palestine was partitioned. The context of their declarations may then be compared with that which currently prevails.

Ben Gurion wrote: "There are two elements — political and spiritual — in the struggle for Jerusalem. They are interdependent, and yet independent of one another. . . . Moreover, our military and economic achievements of the last two years have changed the face of Jerusalem. Both justice and power are on our side in the struggle for Jerusalem. . . . We will succeed in Jerusalem if we show the utmost respect for the rights of our neighbors."[24] The context for this statement was the reaffirmation by

the U.N. General Assembly on December 10, 1949, of the Palestine Partition resolution calling for internationalization of Jerusalem under the aegis of the United Nations. Ben Gurion had
declared on December 13 that the Assembly vote could not and
would not be carried out, "if only for the determined opposition of
the residents of Jerusalem."[25] Instead, he recommended that the
Knesset return to Jerusalem, reaffirming the city's historic position as capital.

'Abdallah's words were: "The demand (by Arab States) for the
internationalization of Jerusalem was the strangest and most
unbalanced of the (Arab) national aims. It was one that disre-
garded the Arab rights and interests by handing over the Holy
Places to international control and wrenching Jerusalem from
the possession of the Arabs. It was my duty to stand resolutely
and firmly in the defense of the Arab character of the Holy City
and resist internationalization in all its aspects. . . . Do they (certain Arab personages) not know that internationalization will
lead to the loss of the Holy City, and Hebron and Nablus as well?
. . . . Umar ibnal-Khattab recognized all the religious and Church
rights of the Christian community. . . . No Muslim ruler has governed Palestine without upholding and preserving the covenant
of Umar."[26]

A quarter of a century ago, these spokesmen for both peoples
rejected internationalization. Each maintained the primacy of
their people's spiritual claim to Jerusalem, as well as assuring
the rights of others. Ben Gurion drew a clear distinction between
the political (international) struggle in the United Nations and
the spiritual struggle of the Jewish people to maintain themselves in Jerusalem. In their references to the spiritual, both Ben
Gurion and 'Abdallah could not completely separate out the
material. Ben Gurion referred to the political pressures exercised
upon the Israeli government by the Jerusalemites. 'Abdallah
pointed out the strategic relationship between Jerusalem and the
hearts of Arab Samaria and Judea.

When Ben Gurion spoke of respecting the rights of neighbors,
the context was the recent terrorism of the Jewish dissidents, and
wartime passions that had just begun to recede. Jewish terrorist
forces had had more freedom to act in Jerusalem than elsewhere,
partly because of the isolation of Jerusalem from central authority controls. The perpetration by IZL (Irgun Zevai Leumi — National Military Organization) of the Dir Yassin massacres on

April 8, 1948, the looting of foreign consulates by IZL as Jewish forces took over West Jerusalem, and the assassination of Count Bernadotte by LEHI were fresh in everyone's mind. Moreover, there was the unresolved question of restitution of property abandoned by Arabs who had fled.

But if the Jews were on the defensive with regard to the rights of others, the Arabs were equally if not more culpable. The Arab destruction of the Old Jewish Quarter on May 28, 1948, wholesale looting of homes and synagogues, desecration of gravestones, tombs and holy scrolls, denial of access to Holy Places were hardly a reassuring backdrop to 'Abdallah's 1951 promises that all religious communities, mosques, churches and synagogues be given their full right.[27] The irony of these promises was brought into sharp relief since nearly all synagogues had already been destroyed during the brief Jordanian rule. Had King 'Abdallah lived, it is possible, though highly unlikely, that his assurances might have been honored. But the nineteen year record of Jordanian control was full of broken promises to Jews, although Christian rights were maintained.

The post 1967 decade of Israel control, in contradistinction, has been one of assurance of Muslim and Christian interests, including complete freedom of access. In retrospect, Ben Gurion's concern for the rights of others must be seen in a far broader context than rights of access to Holy Places. For with reunification of the city, Israel is now addressing itself to the question of how to respect the full socioeconomic and political rights of the country's largest urban Arab minority — the 100,000 Arabs of Jerusalem.

The other context that has changed in the past quarter of a century is the international political arena. Focus is no longer on the United Nations. General Assembly resolutions are discounted in advance by Israel because of the Arab-Communist-Third World's automatic anti-Zionist stance. Instead, the international arena is the one in which the American and Soviet superpowers seek to exercise leverage on the various principals in the conflict. This is generally done on a bilateral basis. The Arab states, while constituting a solid, anti-Israel bloc, nevertheless do not form a solid negotiating front. The most obdurate states in their opposition to any settlement whatsoever are those located in the outermost ring (Libya, Iraq, Algeria) — the "Rejection Front." The inner, or contiguous ring of confrontation states, while at times coming together under joint military command, nevertheless exhibit continuing diversity and shifting in internal alignment.

Over the course of the years, the Palestinian guerrilla movement that operated so freely from bases surrounding Israel (Egypt, Jordan, Syria, Lebanon) has seen those bases either completely closed to them as in Jordan and Egypt, or stringently regulated, as in Syria. In 1975 and 1976, the struggle shifted to Lebanon. As a consequence of the war there, freedom of action is likely to be denied to the PLO in Lebanon as well. Removing guerilla activities farther from the borders of Israel and the West Bank could make it more practical for Palestinians living on the West Bank to shift their arenas of conflict to the diplomatic and political ones. This is not to suggest that they would be prepared to reject the PLO. Indeed, all indications are to the contrary. Rather, they could espouse PLO political objectives, including opposition politics to Israeli occupation, without using PLO military tactics. Involvement of the West Bankers, not so much as alternatives to the PLO, but as political collaborators with the PLO in their opposition to Israeli administration, may lead them eventually to see ideological compromise.

The mediating role that the superpowers can play in the conflict has been narrowed, partly because of military actions between Israel and the Arabs, military action among the Arabs themselves, and substantial changes in the economic balance of the Arab states. These actions have developed a clearer demarcation among the Arabs between national self-interest and pan-Arab ideology. Moreover, they have brought to the forefront the Palestinians of the West Bank and Jordan. Military setbacks by the PLO should not be incorrectly interpreted as diminishing the role of the Palestinians as principals in the solution of the conflict. These setbacks should be appreciated by Israel and the outside powers as offering an opportunity to take ideological contention into the political arena of bilateral negotiation and compromise. Conflict with the Palestinians was the central issue prior to 1967 when Palestinian Arabs had no substantial independent strength. During that period, terrorist activities were regulated by their host countries or were too feeble to require regulation. Loss of the Lebanese base would return the Palestinians to the status quo ante where in each country in which they are located they would be allowed to operate only as the host's political and military circumstances permit. Indeed, now that the Egyptians, Syrians and Jordanians all possess war machines that are substantially more powerful than ever before, Israel's abilities to retaliate against controlled-terrorist actions are likely to be severely circumscribed. This would be especially true if refugee camps were eliminated as PLO training and operational bases, to be replaced by small, hidden and host army-secured centers.

CONCLUSION

The question of the significance of territory in assuring security in the Arab-Israeli conflict is complex. At the level of tactical warfare, a small hill or series of hills, or a ridge or escarpment may be vital. In the Golan Heights fighting of 1973, the surprise Syrian attack swept across the plateau, but could not dislodge by-passed Israeli tanks that took shelter behind hills. From these natural fortresses, advancing Syrian columns were cut down, and the basis for counter-attack was formed. The Golan escarpment overlooking the Hule Valley served as the strong pont for Syrian harassment of Israel prior to 1967, and was a formidable barrier to advancing Israeli troops in the Six Day War. Syrian repossession of these heights through negotiations meets especially adamant opposition from Israel's settlements of the North.

Negotiations over disengagement that found Israelis and Egyptians haggling over the Sinai passes, or Israelis and Syrians arguing about the disposition of three hills threatening Kuneitra but offering protection to Israeli settlement, were not negotiations over negligible issues. In Jerusalem as well, topographical points played vital roles in the fighting of both the War of Independence and the Six Day War. Ammunition Hill, the Abu Tor-Ramat Rahel Ridge, and Nabi Samuil proved points of major tactical value in the fighting.

Strategy for War

In shifting the scale from points to relatively large areas, i.e., from hills and individual farm settlements to the cities, there is a change from the tactical to the strategic. Cities the size of Damascus and Cairo, and even of Suez City and Jerusalem, present considerably more formidable problems for attacking modern armies. More so than individual points, large cities serve as deterrents to war since they eliminate the possibility for probes, feints, and swift seizure of territory. Attacks upon major urban areas in today's Arab-Israeli conflict mean all-out war. They pose the threat that the attacked nation will use all weapons at its command, and that outside powers will intervene directly. More over, such cities make formidable defense structures.

Massed battles within big cities are far more costly to the attackers than are even-pitched battles in open areas, for the latter offer space for maneuvering, breakthroughs, encirclement or retreat. The Israeli caution in attacking Suez City in 1973, after initially experiencing casualties in street fighting in the city outskirts, exemplifies the problem that the city presents to the attacker in war. In this connection, the rapid increase in size and extent of Jerusalem can be viewed as a deterrent to the renewal of war by the Arabs. If war were to come to Jerusalem, it would not only present great difficulties to attacking Arabs, but it would provoke a level of retaliation by Israel that would be speedy and massive, for political as well as military reasons.

From the Israeli standpoint, building up frontier cities like Kiryat Shemoneh, Eilat, Ashkelon, Nahariya, Beisan, Jerusalem and the new city of Yamit at Rafia means building cities that perform this "tripwire" and deterrent function. They are also significant hinges to scattered Jewish agricultural villages in zones of settlement that surround the West Bank, in the Jordan Valley, in the Hebron Hills, in North Sinai and in the Golan. Jerusalem is by far the largest and most significant of these hinges.

Strategy for Peace

A growing unified Jerusalem under Israeli control could decrease the Arab inclinations to renew the conflict on the central front, and would enhance the Israeli military advantage in the event of war. In times of peace, Jerusalem, tied more closely to its metropolitan area and larger city-region, can give to the Arabs a greater degree of political and economic self-confidence. The total metropolitan area including Jerusalem is now almost evenly divided between Jews and Arabs. Certain metropolitan administrative structures could serve as mechanisms for cooperation, without undermining the national powers, controls and safeguards exercised by the sovereignties in either Israel or a Palestinian West Bank political entity.

This volume has dealt with a variety of geopolitical issues and consequences that derive from the contemporary reunification of Jerusalem. From a physical and economic point of view, most impartial observers agree that all parties have benefited in many ways from reunification. The forces that lead to a city's partition, however, seldom are concerned with the physical-economic consequences. The issues in Jerusalem are cultural, social and political. Recognizing that Jews and Arabs have conflicting geopolitical objectives, nevertheless, it is possible to propose political structures and loci for spatial interaction that will provide for some if not all of the vital interests of both peoples.

A major theme is that new geopolitical structures that aim at integrating the two peoples are preferable to structures that reinforce socioeconomic and physical separations and perpetuate a dominant-subordinate relationship. To avoid open discussion and planning for a more equal framework within which the two peoples can co-exist is not to avoid stoking the fires of dissension. Rather, it is to take an ostrich-like stance in a situation which will not indefinitely remain quiescent. Efforts to promote a more geopolitically integrated Jerusalem may increase the short-term risks for dissension and conflict, but will be a long-term stimulus for peace between Arabs and Jews.

Since 1967, rapid and large-scale Jewish settlement in East Jerusalem and the relative decline in population weight of the Old City have promoted Israelization of the city and strengthened the mechanisms and rationale for its political unity. Only vigorous and large-scale measures aimed at spatial integration, however, can assure that Jerusalem's unity will play a greater role in maintaining and enlarging the peace than in triggering conflict. In the absence of positive interactive processes, a disaffected and unassimilable Arab minority in Jerusalem will continue to stand as a major barrier to peace between the two nations.

Since reunification, Israel's formal policy on Jerusalem has been to stand firm on its reunification within Israeli territory, and be receptive to discussions about functional internationalization. Most of the efforts toward integration have been local, led by Jerusalem's mayor, Teddy Kollek, and his aides. While social and cultural interaction is, in the last, analysis, a local, indeed almost a personal matter, the launching of a major drive towards the kinds of spatial integration of Jerusalem that will promote human interaction is a matter of national policy. The Israeli government is the only formal body with the capacity to take action. No other political authority has the capacity or the will to take such initiative. Even though Arabs may consider Israeli initiative as a paternalistic colonialist policy, nevertheless, patient, small-scale, continuing and interconnected efforts by Israel could develop a climate of opinion among the Arabs out of which shared initiative by both peoples can emerge. Opposition will come not only from most Arabs but from those Jews who see the potential success of spatial integration as the death-knell of separation. But repartition of the city, either in its pre-1967 boundaries or in any new ones that might be designed, is an even less desirable option, and would contain even greater seeds for continuing conflict.

A United States policy that favors a united and integrated Jerusalem could be a bold stroke towards peace in the Middle East. The United States is bringing increasing pressure on Israel to return most of the territories taken in 1967. It can only hope to succeed by guaranteeing, in exchange, a united Jerusalem, recognized de jure as Israel's capital.

The current conflict over Jerusalem is first and foremost a territorial struggle between two national peoples — Israelis and Palestinian Arabs. The religious claims of Jews, Muslims and Christians are issues that have to be addressed within the framework of Jewish and Arab nationalism.

Israel could take steps to reassure not only the United States, but also the Christian world (and, to a minor extent, some Muslims) by taking the initiative and formally internationalizing the Holy Places that are Christian and Muslim. It would be timely if Israel were to put into action its frequent proposals on functional internationalization of Jerusalem's churches, monasteries, shrines, cemeteries, mosques and other Holy Places. Just as the Israeli Parliament was able unilaterally to absorb all of Jerusalem within its jurisdiction, so can the Knesset grant extraterritorial status to the Holy Places.[28]

Implementing such steps through unilateral action would be complicated. Who are the legal guardians of each site — the consular corps? religious bodies? Should Jewish Holy Places be included in the same structure of internationalization? Internationalization may not be acceptable to the bodies that are now in conflict over guardianship of some of the Holy Places. There are some political risks for Israel in taking the suggested steps. The advantages of such a bold initiative would, however, be considerable in its impact upon world opinion and American support. It may also put a chink in the Arab armor of distrust. As complicated as carrying out a policy of functional internationalization might be, surely it is less complicated than the concept of internationalizing all of the Old City — a concept that is gaining currency again.[29] The suggested strategy of Israel's taking unilateral action on functional internationalization is the same as the suggestion for unilateral withdrawal from West Bank military government. In both cases it is assumed that the parties, left to their own devices, will develop systems appropriate to their needs.

A major reason cited by the United States in its refusal to recognize Israel's annexation of all of Jerusalem is its concern for the future of the Holy Places.[30] This concern can be dramatically removed by Israel's internationalizing these places on its own initiative. In the interest of achieving a general territorial settlement, it is crucial that the United States recognize the centrality of a unified Jerusalem for Israel. Accepting this fact, the United States can more successfully exert pressures on Israel for territorial concessions elsewhere.

Planning for a co-political, integrated city does not undermine the cause of unity; it supports its rationale and meets the genuine needs of all people concerned. There continues to be a general tendency on the part of Israeli policymakers and the Israeli public to defer the Jerusalem issue until after a framework for peace will have been accepted by Arabs and Jews. This attitude ignores the importance of Jerusalem in the conflict. For Israel to fail to take the initiative on Jerusalem is to invite a policy of Israeli reaction to events fashioned by others — the Arabs or the outside powers. This has led alternately from stalemate and crisis to war; it has not led to peace. Deferring the Jerusalem issue is not deferring the war; it is deferring peace.

FOOTNOTES

1. Matti Golan, *The Secret Conversations of Henry Kissinger, op. cit.,* pp. 93-143.
2. Yehoshafat Harkabbi, Israel's foremost student of the Arab-Israeli conflict writes: "By announcing its readiness to withdraw and let a Palestinian state be set up outside Israel's borders, Israel would return the Palestinian problem to its true natural habitat — inter-Arab politics — and free itself from a heavy burden. By its rejection of a West Bank Palestinian state, Israel has only served the Arab cause very distinguishably, as it has shielded the Arabs from their own devastating contradictions between Jordan and Palestine. Thus, the nature of the regions in the West and East Banks — Hashemite or Palestinian — should be left to the self-determination of the population." Yehoshafat Harkabbi, *Arab Political Strategies and Israel's Response,* from p. 85 of MS copy in press, to be published by the Free Press, Glencoe, Ill., 1976-77.
3. Yeroham Cohen, *Tochnit Allon (The Allon Plan),* (Hebrew), Israel: Hakibbutz Hameuchad Publishing House Ltd., 1972, 189 pp.
4. Bovis entitles the first chapter of his volume, "The Return to Christian Hands," in describing the diplomatic history of the British Mandate. (See H. Eugene Bovis, *The Jerusalem Question, op. cit.,* p. 1).
5. *Ibid.,* pp. 11-13.
6. For succinct reviews of these plans, see Bovis, *ibid.,* pp. 21-44 and Ben Halpern, *The Idea of the Jewish State,* Cambridge: Harvard University Press, 1961, pp. 344-375.
7. In discussing Jerusalem's political and religious problems of the last half century, Bovis states: "Until 1936, it was largely a European question, but from that time on it has been an Arab-Jewish problem as well. In fact, at present, it appears that the Arab-Jewish aspect is the more prominent aspect of the problem. But the Europeans, and indeed people around the whole world, still have an interest in how it is settled." See Bovis, *ibid.,* p. 110.
8. Ben Halpern, *The Idea of the Jewish State, op. cit.,* p. 385. Also see Harry Sacher, *Israel – The Establishment of a State,* London: George Weidenfeld & Nicolson, 1952, pp. 154-180.
9. Official Records of the Second Session of the General Assembly, Supplement No. 11, *United Nations Special Committee on Palestine – Report to the General Assembly, op. cit.,* Vol. I, pp. 47-63, and Vol. II, Map 3.
10. Dov Joseph, *The Faithful City, op. cit.,* p. 217.
11. *Ibid.,* pp. 327-328.
12. *Ibid.,* p. 232.
13. *Ibid.,* p. 268.
14. H. Eugene Bovis, *The Jerusalem Question, op. cit.,* p. 62.
15. *Ibid.,* p. 66. On the next day, September 27, both Foreign Minister Shertok and Prime Minister Ben Gurion informed the Provisional State Council that the Israeli Government would demand of the U.N. General Assembly that the November 29, 1947 Palestine Partition Plan be revised to include Jerusalem as part of the Jewish state (as well as the Negev, the Galilee and the Jerusalem Corridor). The Council approved the government's position. See David Ben Gurion, *Israel: A Personal History, op. cit.,* pp. 271-275.

16. The Bernadotte Plan proposed the following territorial matters:
    1. Inclusion of the whole or part of the Negev in Arab territory.
    2. Inclusion of the whole or part of Western Galilee in Jewish territory.
    3. Inclusion of the City of Jerusalem in Arab territory, with municipal autonomy for the Jewish community and special arrangements for the protection of Holy Places.
    4. Consideration of the status of Jaffa.
    5. Establishment of a free port at Haifa, the area of the free port to include the refineries and terminals.
    6. Establishment of a free airport at Lydda. These proposals were especially favorable to Transjordan which was suggested as the Arab partner in the Union with the Jewish member state. The Arab League rejected the plan at a July 3, 1948 meeting with the Mediator in Cairo, and the Jewish negative reply was transmitted on July 5. (See Folke Bernadotte, *To Jerusalem, op. cit.*, pp. 125-165).

17. On April 7, 1948, Ben Gurion told the Palestine Conciliation Commission of the General Assembly that Israel could not accept a *corpus separatum* for Jerusalem, but would accept an international regime for the Holy Places. This position was reaffirmed by Abba Eban in the Ad Hoc Political Committee on May 5, 1949, with the suggestion that Holy Places be guaranteed — not just in Jerusalem but in all of Palestine. On February 20, 1950, Eban proposed that a U.N. sovereign representative have full control of the Holy Places (all of which lay in Historic Jerusalem, in the eastern sector), with a certain amount of extraterritoriality for these places. See Bovis, *The Jerusalem Question, op. cit.*, pp. 71 and 85. Also, Gabriel Padon, "The Divided City: 1948-1967," in *Jerusalem,* edited by Oesterreicher and Sinai, *op. cit.*, pp. 85-107.

    Meanwhile the General Assembly which had reiterated its support for plans for internationalization of Jerusalem in 1948 and 1949, could not agree to a plan in 1950, and has taken no specific stand since then. See Evan Wilson, *Jerusalem, Key to Peace, op. cit.*, p. 65.

18. David Ben Gurion, *Israel – A Personal History, op. cit.*, pp. 378-79.

19. King 'Abdallah of Jordan, *My Memoirs Completed, op. cit.*, p. 24.

20. *Ibid.,* p. 13.

21. Israel denounced the annexation of Judea and Samaria as "a unilateral act which in no way binds Israel." Foreign Minister Sharett, in making this statement in the Knesset on May 3, 1950, asserted that the Armistice Agreement with Jordan did not constitute a final political arrangement, which would depend upon further negotiations and conclusion of peace. See Yehuda Blum, *Secure Boundaries and Middle Eastern Peace,* Jerusalem: The Hebrew University, Faculty of Law, 1971, pp. 80-91.

22. *Hussein of Jordan: My "War" with Israel, op. cit.*, p. 121.

23. PLO Covenant Article 19 "The partitioning of Palestine in 1947, and the establishment of Israel is fundamentally null and void," and Article 21, "The Palestinian Arab people, in expressing itself through the armed Palestinian Revolution, rejects every solution that is a substitute for a complete liberation of Palestine, and rejects all plans that aim at the settlement of the Palestine issue or its internationalization." Reference to internationalization includes not only Jerusalem, but various suggestions that have been made to place

the West Bank under international administration and protection, as a stage in the evolution of a separate Palestinian West Bank entity. (See Yehoshafat Harkabbi, "The Position of the Palestinians in the Israel-Arab Conflict and their National Covenant," translated by J. Kraemy from *Maariv*, Nov. 4, 1969, p. 13. Also, see *Palestinian National Covenant* as affirmed by the Palestinian National Council, June 10-17, 1968, Cairo).

24. David Ben Gurion, *Israel – A Personal History, op. cit.,* pp. 381-382
25. *Ibid.,* p. 379.
26. King 'Abdallah of Jordan, *My Memoirs Completed, op. cit.,* pp. 13, 66, 77-78.
27. Such a promise was included in 'Abdallah's Diploma of Appointment of Raghib Pasha al-Nashashibi as the new Mufti of Jerusalem, overseer of Haram al-Sharif and High Guardian of the Holy Places, January 5, 1951 (See *Ibid.,* p. 102).
28. On June 27, 1967, the Israeli Parliament took the initiative and approved extension of Israel's laws, jurisdiction and public administration to the Old City and other parts of East Jerusalem that had been under Jordanian control since 1949. On the following day, it took administrative action and extended municipal controls and services over the entire city.
29. Since 1967, the Vatican, the Greek Catholic Patriarch, the Executive Committee of the National Council of Churches, and some Muslim leaders have spoken out for internationalization. For a proposed solution calling for internationalization of the Walled City and the area immediately surrounding it from the Mount of Olives to Mount Zion, see Evan Wilson, *Jerusalem, Key to Peace, op. cit.,* pp. 134-138.

    For a solution that embraces a form of functional internationalization through "Outside Protectors", see H. Eugene Bovis, *The Jerusalem Question, op. cit.,* pp. 122-124.
30. Official U.S. Department of State Policy expressed on June 28, 1967, refuses to recognize "the hasty administrative action . . determining the future of the holy places or the status of Jerusalem *in relation to them*" (author's underlining), and President Johnson is quoted by the department for his June 19, 1967 statement that "there must be adequate recognition of the special interests of three great religions in the holy places of Jerusalem." *Department of State Bulletin,* Vol. LVII, No. 1964, July 17, 1967, p. 60.

Selected Bibliography

King 'Abdallah of Jordan, *My Memoirs Completed,* (al-TaKmilah), translated from the Arabic by Harold W. Glidden, Washington, D.C.: American Council of Learned Societies, 1954.

Yigal Allon, *Shield of David,* Jerusalem: Weidenfeld and Nicolson, 1970.

Gordon Allport, *The Nature of Prejudice,* Cambridge: Addison-Wesley, 1954.

Atlas of Israel, Jerusalem: Survey of Israel, Ministry of Labour and Amsterdam: Elsevier Publishing Company, 1970.

Atlas of Jerusalem, The Israel Academy of Sciences and Humanities, The Israel Exploration Society, The Hebrew University Department of Geography, Jerusalem: Massada Press, 1973.

Abdullah at-Tell, *Karithah Falastin: Mudhakkirat Abdullah at-Tell,* Cairo, 1959, translated into the Hebrew by Yehoshua Halamish, *Zichronot Abd-Allah al-Tall,* Tel Aviv: Maarachot, 1960.

W.H. Bartlett, *Walks About the City and Environs of Jerusalem,* Summer, 1842, reprint, Jerusalem: Canaan Publishing House, 1974.

Yehoshua Ben Arieh, *Eretz Yisrael BaMea HaY"T – Giluya Mehadash (The Rediscovery of the Holy Land in the Nineteenth Century),* (Hebrew), Jerusalem: Carta and the Israel Exploration Society, 1970.

David Ben Gurion *Israel, A Personal History,* translated from the Hebrew by N. Meyers and U. Nystar, New York: Funk & Wagnalls, Inc., 1971.

David Ben Gurion, *Zichronot (Memories),* (Hebrew), Vol. I, Tel Aviv, Am Oved, 1973.

Meron Benvenisti, *Mul HaHoma HaSegura,* (Hebrew), Jerusalem: Weidenfeld and Nicolson, 1973.

Uzi Benziman, *Yerushalayim – Ir L'Lo Homa,* (Hebrew), Tel Aviv: Schocken Publishing House, Ltd., 1973.

Folke Bernadotte, *To Jerusalem,* translated from the Swedish by J. Bulman, London: Hodder and Stoughton, 1951.

Yehuda Blum, *Secure Boundaries and Middle Eastern Peace,* Jerusalem: The Hebrew University, Faculty of Law, 1971.

H. Eugene Bovis, *The Jerusalem Question, 1917-1968,* Stanford: Hoover Institution Press, Stanford University, 1971.

Amnon Cohen, *Palestine in the 18th Century,* Jerusalem: The Magnes Press, The Hebrew University, 1973.

Yeroham Cohen, *Tochnit Allon (The Allon Plan),* (Hebrew), Israel: Hakibbutz Hameuchad Publishing House Ltd., 1972.

Larry Collins and Dominique Lapierre, *O Jerusalem,* New York: Simon and Schuster, 1972.

W.D. Davies, *The Gospel and the Land – Early Christianity and Jewish Territorial Doctrine,* Berkeley: University of California Press, 1974.

East Jerusalem Census of Population and Housing (1966/67), (Hebrew and English), Jerusalem: Central Bureau of Statistics and Jerusalem Municipality, 1968.

Yehuda Erez, editor, *David Ben Gurion – A Pictorial Record,* Tel Aviv: Ayanot Publishing House, 1953.

Walter Eytan, *The First Ten Years,* New York: Simon and Schuster, 1958.

Glubb Pasha, John Bagot, *A Soldier with the Arabs,* London: Hodder and Stoughton, 1957.

Mattl Golan, *The Secret Conversations of Henry Kissinger, Step-by-Step Diplomacy in the Middle East,* translated from the Hebrew by R. and S. Stern, New York: Quadrangle/The New York Times Book Co., 1976

Norman Gosenfeld, *The Spatial Division of Jerusalem, 1948-1969,* Los Angeles: University of California, unpublished Ph.D. dissertation, 1973.

Ben Halpern, *The Idea of the Jewish State,* Cambridge: Harvard University Press, 1961.

Menashe Harel, *Zot Yerushalayim,* (Hebrew), Tel Aviv: Am Oved, 1972.

Yehoshafat Harkabbi, *Arab Political Strategies and Israel's Response,* Glencoe, Ill.: The Free Press (in press).

Hussein of Jordan: *My "War" with Israel,* as told to Vick Vance and Pierre Louer, translated from the French by J.P. Wilson and W.B. Michaels, New York: William Morroco & Co., Inc., 1969.

Avia HaShimshoni, Yosef Shavid, Zion HaShimshoni, *Tochnit-Av Yerushalayim – 1968 (Jerusalem Master Plan),* (Hebrew), Municipality of Jerusalem, with cooperation of Ministry of Housing, Ministry of Transportation, Israel Land Authority and Ministry of Interior, 1974.

Jerusalem, Israel Pocket Library, Jerusalem: Keter Publishing Co., 1973. (compiled from material originally published in the *Encyclopedia Judaica).*

Jerusalem Revealed, Archeology in the Holy City 1968-1974, editor Y. Yadin, translated by R. Grafman, Jerusalem: The Israel Exploration Society in cooperation with Shikmona Publishing Company, 1975.

Jerusalem Through the Ages, (Hebrew), Jerusalem: The Israel Exploration Society, 1968.

Dov Joseph, *The Faithful City – The Siege of Jerusalem, 1948,* New York: Simon and Schuster, 1960.

Josephus, *The Jewish War,* translated from the Latin by G.A. Williamson, London: Penguin, 1959.

Henry Kendall, *Jerusalem, The City Plan: Preservation and Development During the British Mandate, 1918-1948,* London: His Majesty's Stationery Office, 1948.

―――――――――. *The Planning of Jerusalem (Jordan) and Region,* Hashemite Kingdom of Jordan, 1965.

Walid Khalidi, *Jerusalem: The Arab Case,* Amman: Hashemite Kingdom of Jordan, 1967.

Israel Kimchi, Benjamin Heyman, Claud Gabriel, *Yerushalayim, 1967-1975, Sekira Hevratit Kalkalit* (Socio-Economic Survey), (Hebrew), Jerusalem: Hebrew University Institute for Urban and Regional Studies, Jerusalem Studies Center, April, 1976.

Jon and David Kimchi, *Both Sides of the Hill: Britain and the Palestine War,* London: Secker and Warburg, 1960.

Arthur Kutcher, *The New Jerusalem Planning and Politics,* London: Thames and Hudson, Ltd., 1973.

Walter Laqueur, *A History of Zionism,* New York: Holt, Rinehart and Winston, 1972.

Guy Le Strange, *History of Jerusalem Under the Moslems,* reprinted from *Palestine Under the Moslems,* Jerusalem: Ariel Publishing Company (no date).

Netanel Lorch, *The Edge of the Sword: Israel's War of Independence, 1947-49,* New York: G.P. Putnam's Sons, 1951.

Mehoz Yerushalayim, Tochnit Metair Mehozit (Jerusalem District Outline Scheme), (Hebrew), Jerusalem: Ministry of Interior, Planning Department to the Jerusalem District Planning Office, 1972.

Col. Richard Meinertzhagen, *Middle East Diary,* 1917-1956, New York: Thomas Yoseloff, 1959.

John Oesterreicher and Anne Sinai, editors, *Jerusalem,* New York: The John Day Co., 1974.

Stewart Perowne, *The One Remains,* New York: E.P. Dutton & Co., Inc., 1955.

Abraham Rabinovich, *The Battle for Jerusalem, June 5-7, 1967,* Philadelphia: The Jewish Publication Society of America, 1972.

Arthur Ruppin: *Memoirs, Diaries, Letters,* edited by Alex Beinz (translated from the German by Karen Gershon), Jerusalem: Weidenfeld and Nicolson, 1971.

Michael Roman, *Social and Economic Survey of Greater Jerusalem,* Jerusalem: The Morris Falk Institute for Economic Research in Israel, 1967.

Harry Sacher, *Israel – The Establishment of a State,* London: George Weidenfeld & Nicolson, 1952.

George Adam Smith, *The Topography, History and Historical Geography of Jerusalem* (reprinted from 1907), Vol. I, Jerusalem: Ariel Publishing House, (no date).

——————. *History of Jerusalem,* (reprinted from 1907), Vol. II, Jerusalem: Ariel Publishing House, (no date).

Urban Geography of Jerusalem – A Companion Volume to the Atlas of Jerusalem, Jerusalem: Massada Press, 1973.

Zeev Vilnai, *Legends of Jerusalem,* Philadelphia: The Jewish Publication Society of America, 1973.

Yehuda Wallach, *Atlas Karta L'Toldot Eretz Yisrael Mireishit HaHityashvut V'Ad Kom HaMedina,* (Hebrew), Jerusalem: Karta, 1972.

Gideon Weigert, *Israel's Presence in East Jerusalem,* Jerusalem: published by the author, 1973.

Alex Weingrod and R. Mendes-Flohr, *Jewish-Arab Relationships in Jerusalem,* Jerusalem: Jerusalem Studies Center, Hebrew University Institute of Urban and Regional Studies, March, 1976.

Colin Williams, *Jerusalem: A Universal Cultural and Historical Resource,* an Occasional Paper, New York: Aspen Institute for Humanistic Studies, undated.

Col. Sir Charles W. Wilson, *Jerusalem, The Holy City* (reprinted from the book originally published in 1880, under the title *Picturesque Palestine, Sinai and Egypt),* Jerusalem: Ariel Publishing Co., (no date).

Evan M. Wilson, *Jerusalem, Key to Peace,* Washington, D.C.: The Middle East Institute, 1970.

Avraham Wolfensohn, *Bechirot Eizoriot B'Medinat Yisrael,* (Hebrew), Haifa: HaLevanon, 1968.

Articles and Documents

Yehoshua Ben Arieh, "The Old City of Jerusalem," paper presented at the *Association of American Geographers Meeting,* New York City, April, 1975.

Lord Caradon, "The Only Solution," *The Readers Digest,* March, 1975.

Saul Cohen, "Middle East Prospects for Peace," *Jewish Frontier,* April, 1973.
_____ . "Jerusalem: A Geopolitical Imperative," *Midstream,* May, 1975.
_____ . "Geopolitical Bases for the Integration of Jerusalem," *Orbis, A Journal of World Affairs,* Summer, 1976.
Haim Darin-Drabkin, "Jerusalem, City of Dissension or Peace?" *New Outlook, Middle East Monthly,* Vol. 11, No. 1, 1968.
Elisha Efrat, "The Hinterland of the New City of Jerusalem and its Economic Geography," *Economic Geography,* Vol. 40, No. 3, 1964.
Great Britain, *The Palestine Mandate, Parliamentary Papers, 1922* (Cmd. 1785).
_____ . *Palestine, Royal Commission, Report,* London: His Majesty's Stationery Office, 1937 (Cmd. 5479) Peel Report.
_____ . *Palestine, Partition Commission, Report,* London: His Majesty's Stationery Office, 1938 (Cmd. 5854), Woodhead Report.
Yehoshafat Harkabbi, "The Position of the Palestinians in the Israel-Arab Conflict and their National Covenant," translated by J. Kraemy from *Maariv,* Nov. 4, 1969.
The Jerusalem Post, April 30, 1971.
S. Shepard Jones, "The Legal Status of Jerusalem: Some National and International Aspects," *Law and Contemporary Problems,* 33, No. 1, 1968.
Elihu Lauterpacht, *Jerusalem and the Holy Places,* Anglo-Israel Association, Pamphlet No. 19, London: 1968.
Attalah Mansour and Ernest Stock, "Arab Jerusalem After Annexation," *New Outlook, Middle East Quarterly,* Vol. 14, No. 1, 1970.
Menashe Harel, "Massaei David V'HaRomaim B'Maale Adummim," (Hebrew), Nispach L'Hakarat HaAretz, *Maarachot 250,* 1976.
Palestine, Government of, *A Survey of Palestine,* prepared for the Anglo-American Committee of Inquiry, Jerusalem: The Government Printer, 1946.
Palestinian National Covenant, Palestinian National Council, Cairo, June 10-17, 1968.
Don Peretz, "Jerusalem: A Divided City," *Journal of International Affairs,* XVIII, No. 2, 1964.
Abraham Rabinovich, "Plan for Jerusalem," *The Jerusalem Post,* May 7, 1971.
Hayim Moshe Shapira, Minister of Interior, *Askarat Yerushalayim (Harchavat Techum HaIriah)* (Jerusalem Gazette-Expansion of the Municipal Boundary), (Hebrew), June, 1967.
United Nations, Security Council, Official Records, Fourth Year, S/1264/Rev. 1, Special Supplement No. 3: General Armistice Agreement between Egypt and Israel. Lake Success, December 13, 1949. Special Supplement No. 4: General Armistice Agreement between Lebanon and Israel. Lake Success, April 8, 1949. Special Supplement No. 1: General Armistice Agreement between Jordan and Israel. Lake Success, June 20, 1949, and Special Supplement No. 2: General Armistice Agreement between Syria and Israel. Lake Success, June 20, 1949.
United Nations Special Committee on Palestine — Report to the General Assembly, Lake Success, New York: A/364, September 3, 1947, Vol. I, and A/364 Add. 1, September 9, 1947, Vol. II.
United States Department of State *Bulletin,* Vol. LVII, No. 1964, July 17, 1967.
United States Department of State, *Anglo-American Committee of Inquiry, Report to the United States Government and His Majesty's Government in the United Kingdom,* Washington: U.S. Government Printing Office, 1946.

Index